Frommer's™

Lisbon
day BY day™

2nd Edition

by Louise McGrath

WILEY

A John Wiley and Sons, Ltd, Publication

Contents

10 Favorite Moments   1

1 The Best Full-Day Tours   5
The Best in One Day   6
The Best in Two Days   10
The Best in Three Days   16

2 The Best Special-Interest Tours   21
Grand Designs   22
Child's Play: Lisbon with Kids   30
Lisbon's Heroes   34
True Romance   40
Art Club   44

3 The Best Neighborhood Walks   51
The Alfama   52
Avenida-Parque   58
Baixa   62
Cais do Sodré—Chiado—Bairro Alto   66
Belém   70
Rato—Amoreiras—Estrela   74

4 The Best Shopping   77
Shopping Best Bets   78
Lisbon Shopping A to Z   82

5 Lisbon Outdoors   89
Parque Eduardo VII   90
City Center Gardens   92
Parque Florestal de Monsanto & Belém   94

6 The Best Dining 97
Dining Best Bets 98
Lisbon Dining A to Z 103

7 The Best Nightlife 111
Nightlife Best Bets 112
Lisbon Nightlife A to Z 116

8 The Best Arts & Entertainment 123
Arts & Entertainment Best Bets 124
Arts & Entertainment A to Z 127

9 The Best Lodging 131
Lodging Best Bets 132
Lisbon Lodging A to Z 138

10 The Best Day Trips & Excursions 147
Costa do Estoril Beach Hopping 148
Cascais & Estoril 150
Sintra 156

The Savvy Traveler 161
Before You Go 162
Getting There 165
Getting Around 165
Fast Facts 166
Lisbon: A Brief History 170
Useful Phrases 172

Index 175

UK Publisher: Sally Smith
Production Manager: Daniel Mersey
Commissioning Editor: Mark Henshall
Development Editor: Jill Emeny
Project Editor: Hannah Clement
Photo Research: Jill Emeny
Cartography: Tim Lohnes

Wiley also publishes its books in a variety of electronic formats. Some content that appears in print may not be available in electronic books.

British Library Cataloguing in Publication Data

A catalogue record for this book is available from the British Library

ISBN: 978-0-470-74965-4 (pbk), ISBN: 978-0-470-97460-5 (ebk)

Typeset by Wiley Indianapolis Composition Services

Printed and bound in China by RR Donnelley

5 4 3 2 1

A Note from the Editorial Director

Organizing your time. That's what this guide is all about.

Other guides give you long lists of things to see and do and then expect you to fit the pieces together. The Day by Day guides are different. These guides tell you the best of everything, and then they show you how to see it *in the smartest, most time-efficient way*. Our authors have designed detailed itineraries organized by time, neighborhood, or special interest. And each tour comes with a bulleted map that takes you from stop to stop.

Hoping to stroll through the Baixa, explore Lisbon's ancient heart, the Alfama, or enjoy a night out of Portuguese food and fado? Planning a night out in Alcantra, or plotting a day of fun-filled activities with the kids? Whatever your interest or schedule, the Day by Days give you the smartest routes to follow. Not only do we take you to the top attractions, hotels, and restaurants, but we also help you access those special moments that locals get to experience—those "finds" that turn tourists into travelers.

The Day by Days are also your top choice if you're looking for one complete guide for all your travel needs. The best hotels and restaurants for every budget, the greatest shopping values, the wildest nightlife—it's all here.

Why should you trust our judgment? Because our authors personally visit each place they write about. They're an independent lot who say what they think and would never include places they wouldn't recommend to their best friends. They're also open to suggestions from readers. If you'd like to contact them, please send your comments our way at feedback@frommers.com, and we'll pass them on.

Enjoy your Day by Day guide—the most helpful travel companion you can buy. And have the trip of a lifetime.

Warm regards,

Kelly Regan

Kelly Regan, Editorial Director
Frommer's Travel Guides

About the Author

Louise McGrath, a freelance writer and editor, has lived in England, the USA, Colombia, Spain and now Northern Ireland. She's written/updated several guidebooks to Lisbon/Porto, Ireland/Dublin and the English Lake District, as well as dozens of guides worldwide for Whatsonwhen.

Acknowledgments

Thank you to the Lisbon Tourist Office and the Portuguese Tourist Office in London for their continuing support. Thanks also to Frommer's Commissioning Editor Mark Henshall and Editor Jill Emeny for their help and pointers. I am also very grateful to Janet Barradas for keeping me informed about Lisbon's hidden gems. Above all I'd like to thank my husband, Sean McGrath, who took many of the photos in this book and has always given invaluable support.

Dedication

For my husband, Sean.

An Additional Note

Please be advised that travel information is subject to change at any time—and this is especially true of prices. We therefore suggest that you write or call ahead for confirmation when making your travel plans. The authors, editors, and publisher cannot be held responsible for the experiences of readers while traveling. Your safety is important to us, however, so we encourage you to stay alert and be aware of your surroundings.

Star Ratings, Icons & Abbreviations

Every hotel, restaurant, and attraction listing in this guide has been ranked for quality, value, service, amenities, and special features using a **star-rating system.** Hotels, restaurants, attractions, shopping, and nightlife are rated on a scale of zero stars (recommended) to three stars (exceptional). In addition to the star-rating system, we also use a **kids** icon to point out the best bets for families. Within each tour, we recommend cafes, bars, or restaurants where you can take a break. Each of these stops appears in a shaded box marked with a coffee-cup-shaped bullet 🍵.

The following **abbreviations** are used for credit cards:

AE	American Express	DISC	Discover	V	Visa
DC	Diners Club	MC	MasterCard		

Travel Resources at Frommers.com

Frommer's travel resources don't end with this guide. Frommer's website, www.frommers.com, has travel information on more than 4,000 destinations. We update features regularly, giving you access to the most current trip-planning information and the best airfare, lodging, and car-rental bargains. You can also listen to podcasts, connect with other Frommers.com members through our active-reader forums, share your travel photos, read blogs from guidebook editors and fellow travelers, and much more.

A Note on Prices

In the "Take a Break" and "Best Bets" sections of this book, we have used a system of dollar signs to show a range of costs for 1 night in a hotel (the price of a double-occupancy room) or the cost of an entree (main course) at a restaurant. Use the following table to decipher the dollar signs:

Cost	Hotels	Restaurants
$	under $100	under $10
$$	$100–$200	$10–$20
$$$	$200–$300	$20–$30
$$$$	$300–$400	$30–$40
$$$$$	over $400	over $40

How to Contact Us

In researching this book, we discovered many wonderful places—hotels, restaurants, shops, and more. We're sure you'll find others. Please tell us about them, so we can share the information with your fellow travelers in upcoming editions. If you were disappointed with a recommendation, we'd love to know that, too. Please write to:

Frommer's Lisbon Day by Day, 2nd Edition
Wiley Publishing, Inc. • 111 River St. • Hoboken, NJ 07030-5774

10 Favorite
Moments

10 Favorite **Moments**

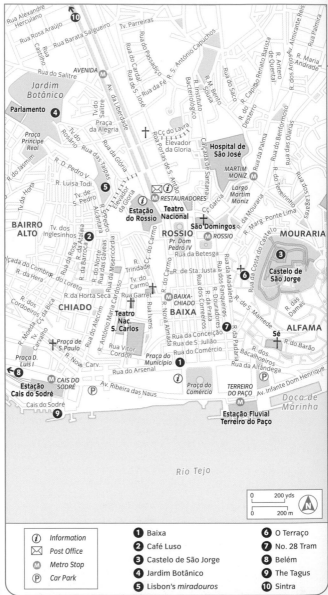

_(i)_ Information

⊠ Post Office

Ⓜ Metro Stop

Ⓟ Car Park

1 Baixa
2 Café Luso
3 Castelo de São Jorge
4 Jardim Botânico
5 Lisbon's *miradouros*

6 O Terraço
7 No. 28 Tram
8 Belém
9 The Tagus
10 Sintra

In the past 20 years Lisbon has opened its doors to the world. Revered for its history and culture, from its famous seafarers and writers to *fado* music, the city has built bridges into the future from the modern Parque das Nações to the revamped Alcântara docks. It all adds up a heady cocktail of art and architecture, vibrant street life, cafe culture, and hip terrace bars.

❶ **Strolling through the Baixa.** At the center of historic Lisbon, the grid of neoclassical streets known as the Baixa is the easiest place to get your bearings. Start at the Lisbon Welcome Center in the Praça do Comércio, and drift through the monumental Arco Triunfal into the bustling Rua Augusta, where street sellers tout souvenirs and paintings. *See p 62.*

❷ **A night of Portuguese food and fado.** When it comes to food and entertainment, the Portuguese know how to put on a good spread. I like to sample the best regional *bacalhau* (salt cod) dishes, skewers of meat and fresh fish at a *fado* restaurant such as **Café Luso** in the Bairro Alto or explore the latest restaurants opening in the arty Santos Design District. *See p 98.*

The Arco Triunfal leads through to the busy Rua Augusta.

Torre de Belém and the River Tejo.

❸ **Exploring the Alfama.** The Alfama is Lisbon's ancient heart, a tangle of cobbled streets and narrow steps. Start by the turrets of the **Castelo de São Jorge** (St George's Castle), taking in the panoramic city views before following the tram tracks down past the cathedral (see p 8). I make a point of rising early on Tuesdays or Saturdays for the *Feira da Ladra* (Thieves Market), a treasure trove of bric-à-brac and painted ceramics. *See p 52.*

❹ **Cooling off in the Botanic Gardens.** I know of no better haven from the summer heat than these lush gardens, between the Bairro Alto and Rato. Stroll under the shade of tall palms, breathing in the scents of orchids and listening to water trickle into the ponds—the city traffic is just a faint buzz. *See p 42.*

5 Taking in the city views from Lisbon's *miradouros*. I never tire of Lisbon's hills: the rewards are the views from the *miradouros* (viewing points). You'll discover your favorites, mine include the Castelo de São Jorge, looking towards the ruined Convento do Carmo; São Pedro de Alcântara, for an Alfama panorama; and the top of Parque Eduardo VII, which looks down its formal gardens and the tree-lined Avenida da Liberdade. *See Castelo de São Jorge, p 8.*

6 Enjoy prized views from a bar terrace at night. Already spoiled with panoramic views from the miradouros, now *Lisboetas* want to enjoy them with a drink on one of the many bar terraces. You'll find them overlooking the River Tagus waterfront, but the higher up, the more fashionable it is, especially rooftop bars like **O Terraço** in the Baixa and hillside terraces in the ancient Alfama. *See p 116.*

7 Riding the No. 28 Tram. Whether your feet can take the cobbled hills or not, this is still a great way to see Lisbon's oldest districts. The old red tram creaks and

trundles up and down the hills from the Alfama through the Baixa to the Bairro Alto and on to Estrela and Campo de Ourique. *See p 7.*

8 The Manueline architecture of Belém. The Mosteiro dos Jerónimos (Jerónimos Monastery) and Torre de Belém (Belém Tower) are the pinnacles of Portuguese architecture. These structures are full of clues—such as carved ropes and sculptures of monarchs—reflecting Portugal's Golden Age of Discovery, when its seafarers stepped out on a voyage of exploration that changed the world. *See p 24.*

9 The Tagus at sunset. You can walk along the riverside pathway from Cais do Sodré, past the Alcântara docks, cafes, and restaurants, continuing under the 25 de Abril Bridge and onto Belém. Groups of joggers trot the route and enjoy the sunset or if preferred, you can cycle the entire 12km. *See p 10.*

10 Immersing yourself in Sintra's fantasy. Lord Byron's description of Sintra's royal palaces and their mountain setting as a 'Glorious Eden' is close to the truth. There are two main palaces: one in the town, the other a romantic creation on a hilltop, with far-ranging views. *See p 156.* ●

Palácio Nacional da Pena in Sintra.

1 The Best **Full-Day Tours**

The Best **in One Day**

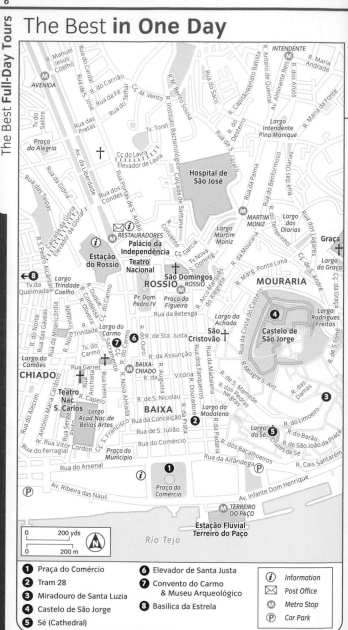

1	Praça do Comércio	**6**	Elevador de Santa Justa
2	Tram 28	**7**	Convento do Carmo & Museu Arqueológico
3	Miradouro de Santa Luzia	**8**	Basílica da Estrela
4	Castelo de São Jorge		
5	Sé (Cathedral)		

- *(i)* Information
- ✉ Post Office
- Ⓜ Metro Stop
- Ⓟ Car Park

This full-day tour gives you a rich and concise introduction to Lisbon's historic center and avoids traveling any great distance. It follows part of the route of the most celebrated of Lisbon's rickety old trams—the No.28. Start early to beat the crowds and take in the individual districts of Alfama, Baixa, Chiado, Bairro Alto, and Estrela. START: **Praça do Comércio. Metro: Baixa/Chiado. Tram: 12, 15. Bus: 2, 81, 92, 711, 713.**

❶ ★ Praça do Comércio. This stately neoclassical square (*praça*) faces the River Tagus (Rio Tejo) on one side and the grid of streets that make up the Baixa Pombalina on the inland side. The square is usually my first port of call. A recent re-vamp has enhanced the square's architecture and facilitated access to the waterfront. The re-design has also kept the 18th-century bronze statue at the center of the square. A prominent symbol of power, this depicts Dom José I (1714–77), king at the time of Lisbon's great earthquake. Use the square as a starting point, picking up information and tourist discount cards from the **Lisbon Welcome Center**. Several sightseeing tour buses, trams, and buses also stop here. The **Arco Triunfal** (Triumph Arch, see p 62) marks the entrance to the Baixa's pedestrian street, **Rua de Augusta**, which buzzes with street sellers, artists, and tourists. ⏱ *20 min. Metro: Baixa-Chiado. Tram: 15, 18, 25. Bus: 2, 81, 92, 711, 713.*

❷ ★★★ kids Tram 28. I regularly use this tram, a popular route with tourists as it links several of the city's historic districts. Although Lisbon is generally a safe city, the tram is renowned for pickpockets. Don't let that spoil your enjoyment: just keep valuables tucked away and enjoy the ride as the tram clanks along the cobbled streets. ⏱ *10 min. Eastbound Mon–Fri 6:20am–11:20pm, Sat 6:15am–11:05pm, Sun 7:25am–11:05pm. Westbound Mon–Fri 5:40am–11:10pm, Sat 5:45am–10:35pm, Sun 6:45am–10:35pm.*

Praça do Comércio, a great place to start your tour.

Tram 28, which links several of the city's historic districts.

Services every few minutes. 1.40€ single.

❸ ★ Miradouro de Santa Luzia. One of the city's most famous *miradouros*, this looks over the steep Alfama district and down towards the Tagus. I like to linger over a coffee here and take in the views. It's also located by the access road up to the castle. Stop at the small **Igreja de Santa Luzia** (see p 55, **❿**), and note the antique tiled panel opposite the church, depicting a rather less developed city panorama. ⏲ *20 min. Tram: 12, 28. Bus: 37.*

❹ ★★★ Castelo de São Jorge. An archway marks the entrance to this castle; continue up the cobbled slope to buy your tickets at the Casa do Gobernador (Governor's House). The barriers to the left of the house lead into a leafy square, Praça das Armas, with its mighty statue of Dom Afonso Henriques (1109–85), Portugal's first king and liberator from Moorish rule.

Built in or around the 10th century by the Moors as a means of defense, the castle was extended as a Royal Palace from the 13th to 16th centuries, but fell into neglect after the royal family moved to what is now the **Praça do Comércio**. Very little of the original structure remains, but 20th-century reconstruction evokes something of what it was. The large leafy square offers spectacular city views, and the inner courtyard of the castle often echoes to the sounds of musicians playing, as you climb the towers. ⏲ *1–1½ hr. Alfama.* ☎ *21-880-0620. www. castelosaojorge.egeac.pt. Admission 5€, 30% discount Lisboa Card, free under 10s & seniors. Nov–Feb 9am–6pm; Mar–Oct 9am–9pm.*

❺ ★ Sé (Cathedral). I like to follow the tram tracks downhill on foot to take in the atmosphere of the Alfama district. Built on the site of an old mosque in the 12th century, the cathedral has been altered over time. At first I found the interior dark and austere, but once my eyes had adjusted, I found certain details quite appealing. Look out for the decorated capitals of the main portal, with carved figures of the Archangel Michael and fighting men mounted on strange beasts, and the vaulted ceilings of the main nave and ambulatory. The impressive

Gothic tombs and cloisters with double arches are also worth a visit. ⏱ *20–45 min. Largo da Sé.* ☎ *21-886-6752. Free admission; cloisters 2.50€. Daily 9am–7pm; cloisters Oct–Apr only, Mon–Sat 10am–6pm, Sun 2–6pm. Tram: 12, 28. Bus: 37.*

⑥ ★★ Elevador de Santa Justa. The tram track trundles back down into the heart of the Baixa, kinder on the feet than the cobbled hills of the Alfama. At the western end of Rua Santa Justa is the eye-catching iron Santa Justa elevator, built by engineer Raoul Mesnier du Ponsard in 1898–1901, to transport people to the streets above (it still works). At the top there's a cafe with great views of the Baixa, Rossio Square (see p 64), and the castle. ⏱ *10–30 min. Rua de Santa Justa. Admission 2.80€ or free with Carris travel pass. Winter daily 7am–9pm; summer daily 7am–11pm. Metro: Baixa-Chiado, Rossio. Tram: 15, 28. Bus: 2, 9, 36, 37, 44, 81, 92.*

⑦ ★★★ Convento do Carmo & Museu Arqueológico. The convent, originally dating back to the 14th century, stands as an eerily majestic monument to the 1755 earthquake. Once inside the roof-less ruins tower above like dinosaur bones. There is a wealth of archeological exhibits, including ancient Jewish gravestones, an Egyptian sarcophagus, and baroque tiled panels, but its contemplative air is what grabs me: sit on the steps and take in the whole scene. ⏱ *45 min–1 hr. Largo do Carmo, 4.* ☎ *21-346-0473. Admission 2.50€, 1.50€ students & seniors; free under 14s & public holidays until 2pm. May–Sep Mon–Sat 10am–6pm; Oct–Apr Mon–Sat 10am–5pm.*

⑧ ★★ Basílica da Estrela. Tram 28 stops directly outside this basilica, built shortly after the earthquake, in 1779, by the queen Dona Maria I (1734–1816), who is entombed here. The two white bell towers and dome make it one of Lisbon's great landmarks, with the figures above the four columns of the façade representing faith, adoration, liberty, and gratitude. Inside the church you'll find paintings by Italian masters against a back drop of pink, white, and black marble. ⏱ *30 min–1 hr. Largo da Estrela.* ☎ *21-396-0915. Free admission. Daily 8am–8pm. Tram: 28.*

The towering skeleton of Convento do Carmo destroyed in the 1755 earthquake.

The Best **in Two Days**

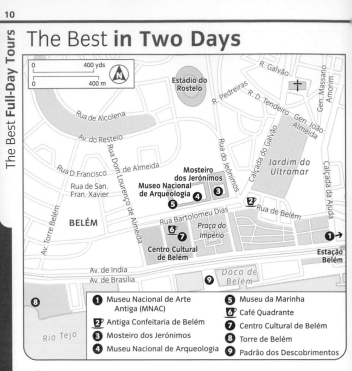

1. Museu Nacional de Arte Antiga (MNAC)
2. Antiga Confeitaria de Belém
3. Mosteiro dos Jerónimos
4. Museu Nacional de Arqueologia
5. Museu da Marinha
6. Café Quadrante
7. Centro Cultural de Belém
8. Torre de Belém
9. Padrão dos Descobrimentos

After spending a day exploring the oldest part of Lisbon, this tour introduces you to one of Lisbon's most iconic areas, venturing west along the Tagus to Belém. Start early to enjoy a couple of hours in the Museu Nacional de Arte Antiga on the way, taking the rest of the day to explore Belém. Note you'll need to take a bus or tram: it's too far to walk for most. START: **Museu Nacional de Arte Antiga. Tram: 15, 18, 25. Bus: 6, 28, 60, 713, 714, 727, 794.**

1 ★★★ Museu Nacional de Arte Antiga (MNAC). Allocate plenty of time to do justice to Portugal's most valuable art collection, housed in a 17th-century palace (with an extension on the site of an older Carmelite convent). You can see the entire collection in a brisk couple of hours, or make a beeline for the prized collection of Portuguese religious paintings and sculpture from the 15th and 16th centuries. Also seek out the baroque chapel on the first floor,

the only part of the convent that remains. If you've time to spare, take in the varied displays of jewelry, ceramics, and furniture from France, Portugal, and former colonies. ⏱ *1–1½ hr. Rua das Janelas Verdes.* ☎ *21-391-2800. www.mn arteantiga-ipmuseus.pt. Admission 4€, 60% discount youth card holders, 50% discount 15–25 years & seniors, free under 14s and on Sun and public holidays. Tues 2–6pm, Wed–Sun 10am–6pm. Tram: 15, 28. Bus: 6, 28, 60, 713, 714, 727, 794.*

The Golden Age of Discovery

Portugal's most prominent period of maritime exploration took place during the 15th and 16th centuries, with the aim of finding new trade and Christianizing the Muslims to the south. The Infante Dom Henrique, better known as Henry the Navigator (1394–1460), led the first push beginning with his expedition to the Moroccan city of Céuta in 1415. Further explorations sailed south along the west African coast, and in 1487 Bartolomeu Dias (1450–1500) made it round the Cape of Good Hope. A little over a decade later, Vasco da Gama (1460–1524) crossed the Indian Ocean, bypassing the arduous overland Silk Road and fueling the spice trade. In 1500 Pedro Alvares Cabral 'discovered' Brazil, and in 1519 Fernão de Magalhães (1480–1521) set out to find a western route to the Indonesian spice islands. Funded by the Spanish, he is better known as Ferdinand Magellan. He reached the Philippines but died there in 1521.

2 **Antiga Confeitaria de Belém.** When you alight from the tram, cross the road to this cafe, recognizable by the blue canopies. Queue at the counter for a quick coffee and one of their famous delicious pasteis de Belém (custard tarts), or slip into one of the tiled back rooms for waiter service. *Rua de Belém, 84–92.* ☎ 21-363-7423. $–$$

3 ★★★ **Mosteiro dos Jerónimos.** A national icon, this monastery constantly strikes me for its size and delicate carved details. Built on the orders of Dom Manuel I, in the 16th century, it is considered one of the most important examples of Manueline architecture (see p 24). The monastery is at its best during Mass, but as soon as it's finished the crowds pour through the door. It tends to be quieter towards the end of the day.

Carved ceiling of the Mosteiro dos Jerónimos.

Mosteiro dos Jerónimos

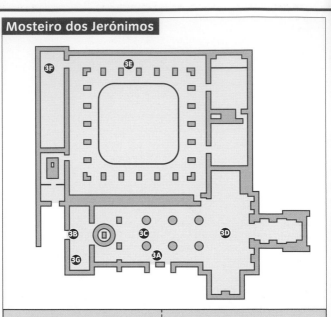

The **3A** **south portal** is the visual centerpiece of the exterior, with elaborate carvings of the Virgin of Belém (Bethlehem) surrounded by angels, rich floral details, and scenes from the life of São Jerónimo. At the **3B** **main portal,** look out for the intricate figurines of Dom Manuel I and his queen, Dona Maria, and scenes from the birth of Christ.

Inside, the **3C** **church** has three naves and the ornate tombs of explorer Vasco da Gama (1460–1524) and writer Luis de Camões (1524–80). The main nave's vaulted ceiling is supported by just six columns, entwined with characteristic Manueline carved ropes and exotic flora). At the far end is the **3D** **capela-mor,** the main chapel, built for (the queen) Dona Catarina

in 1571 with panels of Mannerist paintings.

For me the **3E** **cloisters** decorated with Manueline carvings and the **3F** **refectory** walls lined with 17th-century *azulejos* (tiled) panels are the real highlights. Look out for the tomb of writer Fernando Pessoa (1888–1935). Upstairs in the **3G** **choir,** you can take in the church from above and admire the carved stalls. ⏱ *30 min–1 hr. Praça do Império.* ☎ *21-362-0034. www. mosteirojeronimos.pt. Admission cloisters 6€, 3€ seniors, 2.40€ youth card holders, free under 15s, general public Sun & public holidays until 2pm. Oct–Apr Tues–Sun 10am– 5pm; May–Sept Tues–Sun 10am– 6pm. Train: Belém. Tram: 15. Bus: 27, 28, 29, 43, 49, 51.*

④ ★★ Museu Nacional de Arqueologia. You can either enter this archeology museum through the door opposite the main portal of the church or through the main entrance at the front of the building. Often ignored by visitors who dash off to lunch after seeing the church and cloisters, there are various treasures here dating from the Paleolithic to medieval periods Highlights include some near-complete Roman mosaics as well as elaborate Egyptian funerary masks. ⏰ *45 min–1 hr. Praça do Império.* ☎ *21-362-0000. www.mnarqueologia-ipmuseus.pt. Admission 4€, 2€ 15–25 years, students & seniors; free under 15s, Lisboa Card, general public Sun 10am–2pm. Tues–Sun 10am–6pm. Train: Belém. Tram: 15. Bus 27, 28, 29, 43, 49, 51, 112.*

⑤ ★ Museu da Marinha. At the far end of the former monastery, the Maritime Museum is the place to learn about Portugal's significant relationship with the sea. From a typical Manueline vaulted entrance hall, you are introduced to the first explorers and then taken on a journey through seafaring history, including the Golden Age of Discovery as well as naval ships, merchant sailing, fishing, and royal vessels. There's information in English en route, but if time's limited, head for the highlights: objects from the Far East, such as porcelain and frightening Samurai swords; and the Pavilhão das Galeotas, a large pavilion with life-size models of royal boats, fishing and other craft. ⏰ *45 min–1 hr. Praça do Império.* ☎ *21-362-0019. Admission 4€, 2€ kids 6–17, students & seniors, 2. 50€ Lisboa Card, free under 6s & general public Sun 10am–1pm. Oct–Apr Tues–Sun 10am–5pm; May–Sept Tues–Sun 10am–6pm. Train: Belém. Tram: 15. Bus: 27, 28, 29, 43, 49, 51, 112.*

⑥ ★ Café Quadrante. A useful budget option for a quick lunch, inside the Belém Cultural Center. It's self-service and offers soups, salads, and quiches as well as hot international dishes. *Avenida de Brasília.* ☎ *21-362-0865. Centro Cultural de Belém, Praça do Império.* ☎ *21-362-9256. $.*

The ornate south portal of the Mosteiro dos Jeronimos.

7 ★★★ **Centro Cultural de Belém.** The Belém Cultural Center's sleek, modern form is not to everyone's taste, but that's part of what I like about it. To me it's a monumental and forward-looking statement that respects the older constructions around it. This has become one of the most vibrant cultural centers in the country for contemporary music and the performing arts (see p 127). It hosts temporary exhibitions by renowned modern artists and is the permanent home of the **Museu Berardo, Colecção de Arte Moderno e Contemporâneo** (see p 46, **3**). The collection is displayed on rotation by art movement or theme, from Surrealism to Pop Art and Postmodernism. The cafe and restaurant are great for lunch, with a reasonably priced buffet and a balcony overlooking Belém and the river. There's also a well-stocked wine store and a bookshop offering many art titles. ⏱ *30 min–1 hr. Praça do Império.* ☎ *21-361-2400. www.ccb.pt. www. museuberardo.com. Free admission. Museum daily 10am–7pm (Sat until 10pm). Train: Belém. Tram: 15. Bus: 27, 28, 29, 43, 49, 51, 112.*

8 ★★★ **kids Torre de Belém.** Along with the Mosteiro dos Jerónimos, the Belém Tower is a UNESCO World Heritage Site and another superb example of Manueline architecture. Built in the 16th century to defend the city, the monument looks out along the river to the sea. It stands out on its own but despite the walk along the busy Avenida de Brasília, it's a relaxing place with a shaded park leading to benches on the waterfront. Take in the castellated tower from the outside with carvings of ropes, regal domes, shields, and intricate balconettes with the cross of the Knights of Christ. You can see along the river from the balcony but climb the steps to the top of the tower for more impressive views and to admire carved coats of arms, flora, and animal heads. ⏱ *30–45 min. Avenida de Brasília.* ☎ *21-362-0034. Admission 4€, 2€ seniors, 1.60€ youth card holders; free under 15s & general public Sun & public holidays until 2pm. Oct–Apr Tues–Sun 10am–5pm; May–Sept Tues–Sun 10am–6:30pm. Train: Belém. Tram: 15. Bus: 27, 28, 29, 43, 49, 51, 112.*

The Centro Cultural de Belém.

The Torre de Belém.

⑨ ★★★ Padrão dos Descobrimentos. The 50m-high Discoveries Monument is an aptly shaped homage to Portugal's Golden Age of Discovery and a great place to end your day's tour. First built in 1940 by architect José Cotinelli Telmo and sculptor Leopoldo de Almeida as part of the Portuguese World Exhibition, it was reconstructed in concrete in 1960 to mark the fifth centenary of Henry the Navigator's death. From the side you can see it represents a *caravela* (Portuguese explorers' boat) and from the bow to the stern, it is lined with major figures of the Discoveries, from Henry the Navigator and Vasco da Gama to Luis Vaz de Camões and Nuno Gonçalves. You have to pay to go inside where you'll find a viewing platform and exhibitions, but you can see the outside for free any time. ⏱ *20 min. Avenida de Brasília.* ☎ *21-303-1950. www.padraodescobrimentos.egeac.pt. Admission to viewing platform and exhibitions 2.50€, 1.50€ kids 12–18, students under 25, seniors, free under 12s, 30% discount Lisboa Card. Oct–Apr Tues–Sun 10am–6pm; May–Sept Tues–Sun 10am–7pm. Train: Belém. Tram: 15. Bus: 27, 28, 29, 43, 49, 51, 112.*

Padrão dos Descobrimentos, homage to Portugal's golden age of discovery.

The Best **in Three Days**

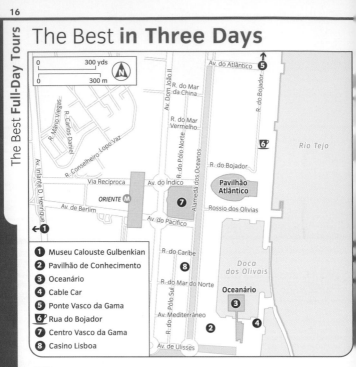

```
0        300 yds
0        300 m
```

Av. do Atlântico **5**

R. do Mar
da China

R. do Mar
Vermelho

Rio Tejo

R. Mário Viegas

R. Carlos Daniel

R. Conselheiro Lopo Vaz

Av. Infante D. Henrique

Via Recíproca

ORIENTE Ⓜ

Av. de Berlim

←**1**

Av. Dom João II

R. do Pólo Norte

Alameda dos Oceanos

Av. do Índico

Av. do Pacífico

R. do Bojador

Pavilhão
Atlântico

R. do Bojador

Rossio dos Olivias

7

6⚲

Museu Calouste Gulbenkian ①
Pavilhão de Conhecimento ②
Oceanário ③
Cable Car ④
Ponte Vasco da Gama ⑤
Rua do Bojador ⑥⚲
Centro Vasco da Gama ⑦
Casino Lisboa ⑧

R. do Caribe

R. do Mar do Norte

8

Oceanário

3

R. do Pólo Sul

Av. Mediterrâneo

R. do Pólo Sul

2

4

Av. de Ulisses

Doca
dos Olivias

During the first two days you would have seen some of
Lisbon's most iconic attractions, but with an extra day you
have the chance to spend time at the eclectic Gulbenkian Museum
and Garden, visit the city's modern district of Parque das Nações,
and enjoy some shopping and entertainment. **START: Praça do Comércio. Metro Baixa-Chiado. Tram: 12, 15. Bus: 2, 81, 92, 711, 713.**

**① ★★★ Museu Calouste
Gulbenkian.** The eclectic collection at the Gulbenkian Museum is a
treasure trove of art brought
together by Calouste Sarkis Gulbenkian, after whom the museum is
named. You could spend all morning here so make an early start and
plan your visit; choose from Oriental, Classical, or European Art or
cherry-pick from each section.
Gulbenkian was particularly

*Museum Calouste Gulbenkian across its
lush gardens.*

passionate about Eastern Islamic Art, so this is definitely a highlight of the gallery, along with the paintings and sculptures by European masters (see p 48). If you have time, relax outside for 10 minutes in the gardens, which are a lush mix of greenery, water features, and some superb sculptures. ⏱ 1–3 hr. *Avenida de Berna, 45A.* ☎ *21-782-3000. www.museu.gulbenkian.pt. Admission 4€, 20% discount Lisboa Card; 50% discount seniors & students, free under 12s. Tues–Sun 10am– 5:45pm. Metro: São Sebastião, Praça de Espanha. Bus: 16, 26, 31, 46, 56.*

❷ **Pavilhão de Conhecimento.** The Knowledge Pavilion is one for the kids, an interactive science center aimed at introducing children to everything from the natural elements to the workings behind our own abilities, and senses. *Alameda dos Oceanos;* ☎ *21-891-7100. www.pav conhecimento.pt. Admission 7€, 4€ seniors & 7–17 yrs, 3€ 3–6 yrs, free under 3 yrs, 15€ families (1 or 2*

adults with children up to 17 years). Tues–Fri 10am–6pm; weekends and bank holidays 11am–7pm. Metro & Trains: Oriente; Bus: 5, 10, 19, 21, 28, 50 ,68, 81, 82, 85.

❸ ★★★ **kids Oceanário.** The Oceanarium is one of the most expensive attractions in the city, but definitely worth the entrance fee. You follow the arrows through four biospheres, first above water and then below. Between each habitat is the Global Ocean where you'll come face to face with sharks, groupers, stingray, and the big (but hardly graceful), one-ton sun fish. Each of the four habitats has the temperature, lighting, flora and fauna of its geographic region, so in the North Atlantic you'll see puffins and razorbills above water and anemones, jellyfish, rocky reefs, and sea grassbeds below.

Oceanário's Mascot.

⏱ 1–1½ hr. *Doca dos Olivais.* ☎ *21-891-7002. www.oceanario.pt. Admission 12€, 6.50€ seniors, 6€ kids 4–12, free under 3s, 29€ families (2 adults/2 children under 13 yrs).*

Calouste Sarkis Gulbenkian (1869–1955)

Born in Istanbul to a wealthy Armenian merchant family, Gulbenkian studied in Marseilles and London before making his own fortune in gasoline. He became an avid art collector, accumulating a large number of Islamic objects as well as painting, sculpture, and decorative art by European masters. He came to Lisbon during WWII and resided here until his death in 1955. He donated a number of important works to the Museu Nacional de Arte Antiga from 1949–52, and in his will requested the creation of a foundation in his name to house his huge collection of art.

Parque das Nações: An Overview

Built for Expo '98, Nations' Park is an ultra-modern district. It might not be to everyone's taste, but you have everything you need in a clean and open space, which can be enjoyed at your own pace. I love everything from the Discoveries theme of the tiled panels in the **metro station** and the palm-tree effect of the **Oriente train station** to the curious scattering of sculptures, and the **Portuguese Pavilion,** its curved roof a masterpiece of architecture and engineering. Then there are the spectacular views of the **Vasco da Gama Bridge.** I'll happily wander on foot from one end to the other but alternatively, you can hop on a **tourist train,** hire a bike **at the facility** by the Oceanarium, or take a **cable car.** With little traffic, plenty of family-friendly eateries (see p. 99) and attractions, the park is perfect for kids. You can buy a Park Card *(Cartão do Parque)* from the Information Spot *(Posto de Informação)* opposite the shopping center (17.50€, 9€ kids 4–12 and over 65s), which gives you free entry to the Oceanário, Pavilhão de Conhecimento, cable car, and mini-train. *Parque das Nações. www.portaldasnacoes.pt. Metro: Vasco da Gama. Bus: 5, 25, 28, 44, 708, 750, 759, 794.*

Apr–Oct daily 10am–7pm, Nov–Mar daily 10am–6pm, 25 Dec 1pm–6pm, New Year's Day Noon–6pm. Metro & Train: Oriente. Bus: 5, 25, 28, 44, 708, 750, 759, 794.

❹ ★ kids Cable Car. If you don't mind heights (and the occasional wobble during windy weather), then hop on the cable car for a bird's-eye view. Starting south of the

Ponte Vasco da Gama bridge.

Families can take advantage of the tourist train in Parque das Nações.

Oceanarium, you'll appreciate the vast width of the river on one side and look across the Pavilhão Atlântico, exhibition center, and restaurants below you on the left. If you enjoy a walk, just buy a single ticket and take time to have lunch or a drink at the dozens of restaurants on the way back to the metro. ⏱ *10–15 min. Between Doca dos Olivais and Torre de Vasco da Gama.* ☎ *21-895-6143. www.portaldasnacoes.pt. Admission 3.90€ one way, 6€ round trip, 2€ kids 5–14 & seniors one way, 3.30€ kids 5–14 & seniors round trip, free under 5s. Oct–May Mon–Fri 11am–7pm; Sat, Sun and public holidays 10am–8pm; Jun–Sept Mon–Fri 11am–8pm; Sat, Sun and public holidays 10am–9pm. Metro & Train: Oriente. Bus: 5, 25, 28, 44, 708, 750, 759, 794*

⑤ ★ Ponte Vasco da Gama. The Vasco da Gama Bridge opened in time for Expo '98, and is the longest bridge in Europe, measuring an impressive 17.2km, around 12km of which cross the Tagus. To me it represents a connection between the city's past and future. Named after one of its most famous

explorers, the bridge crosses the water in a new direction, providing pan-European trade routes. ⏱ *5 min. Metro: Oriente. Bus: 5, 25, 28, 44, 708, 750, 759, 794.*

⑥ Rua do Bojador. More of a strip than a street, this is a long line of restaurants beside Lisbon's exhibition center, facing the Garcia Horta gardens and the river beyond. Choose from an impressive choice of cuisines, from traditional Portuguese and specialist fish restaurants to Spanish tapas, Italian, Irish, and more. Many have terraces for eating alfresco and others transform from family restaurants to discos and karaoke clubs at night. *$–$$$.*

⑦ Centro Vasco da Gama. This convenient indoor shopping center has train and metro lines below and, in usual Portuguese style, a varied selection of eateries. There's everything here from high-street fashion favorites to trendy homeware, and a supermarket where you can buy some typical Portuguese goodies to take home. There's also a multiplex cinema showing all the latest

Outdoor Art in Parque das Nações

One of the things I love about the Nations' Park is the attention to detail. Scattered around are works of art inspired by myths and legends, each one bringing the district to life. Two iron sculptures are among the most striking, and my own personal favorites: *Rhizome* by Antony Gormley (outside the Portuguese Pavilion) is a collection of legs and torsos balanced in an impossible acrobatic pose, and *Homem—Sol* by Jorge Viera opposite the Vasco da Gama shopping center is a spiky metal cactus, almost human in form. Also see the *Rio Vivo*, a three-part mosaic inspired by fish, in Passeio Neptuno made from Italian tesserae by Rolando Sá Nogueira, and Pedro Proença's Portuguese stone pavement in Cais dos Argonautos depicting *Monstros Marinhos*, marine monsters as they were imagined in the Middle Ages.

blockbuster films in English with Portuguese subtitles, so restless kids should be well entertained and fed here. ⏱ *30 min–2 hr. Avenida João II.* ☎ *21-893-0601. www.centro vascodagama.pt. Daily 10am–Midnight. Metro & Train: Oriente. Bus: 5, 25, 28, 44, 708, 750, 759, 794.*

8 Casino Lisboa. A large, sleek, black and mirrored building, the casino offers gaming (slots, blackjack, poker, and more), glamorous shows by international performers, restaurants, and bars. ⏱ *30 min plus. Alameda dos Oceanos. www. casinolisboa.pt. Sun–Thurs 3pm–3am, Fri, Sat and public holiday evenings 4pm–4am. Metro: Oriente. Bus: 5, 25, 28, 44, 708, 750, 759, 794.* ●

Vasco da Gama shopping center.

Grand Designs

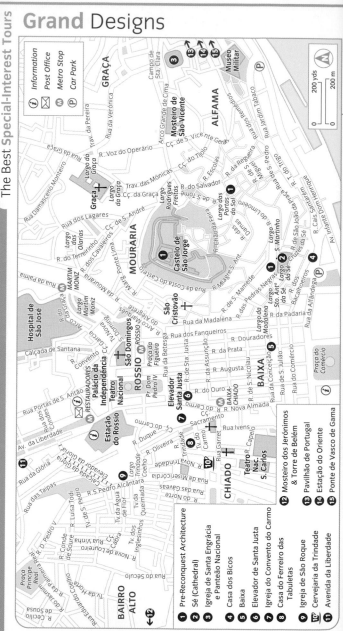

Legend:
- ⓘ Information
- ☒ Post Office
- Ⓜ Metro Stop
- Ⓟ Car Park

0 — 200 yds
0 — 200 m

Map labels:

GRAÇA
ALFAMA
Museu Militar
Campo de Sta. Clara
Mosteiro de São Vicente
MOURARIA
Castelo de São Jorge
São Cristóvão
Hospital de São José
MARTIM MONIZ
Largo Martim Moniz
ROSSIO
São Domingos
Palácio da Independência
Teatro Nacional
Praça da Figueira
Pr. Dom Pedro IV
Estação do Rossio
BAIXA
Elevador Santa Justa
BAIXA-CHIADO
CHIADO
Teatro Nac. S. Carlos
Praça do Comércio
BAIRRO ALTO

Numbered list:

1. Pre-Reconquest Architecture
2. Sé (Cathedral)
3. Igreja de Santa Engrácia e Panteão Nacional
4. Casa dos Bicos
5. Baixa
6. Elevador de Santa Justa
7. Igreja do Convento do Carmo
8. Casa do Ferreiro das Tabuletas
9. Igreja de São Roque
10. Cervejaria da Trindade
11. Avenida da Liberdade
12. Mosteiro dos Jerónimos & Torre de Belém
13. Pavilhão de Portugal
14. Estação do Oriente
15. Ponte de Vasco da Gama

This tour introduces you to Lisbon's distinctive buildings, representing some of the most prominent architectural styles in the city from the Reconquest to the present day. It's not always practical to see them in chronological order, but by the end of the tour you should have a snapshot of the city's turbulent history and occupants through the architectural additions they made. **START: Miradouro de Santa Luzia. Tram: 12, 28. Bus: 37.**

❶ ★ Pre-Reconquest Architecture. The Romans fortified Lisbon from the 3rd century B.C., but the only evidence of their occupation remains at the **Museu do Teatro Romano** (p 56), near the cathedral. Along with the help of a multimedia show, this highly informative, compact museum shows you what the Roman theater actually looked like (p 56). There's virtually no Moorish architecture (denoting buildings erected by Moors, or Muslims of north African origin) either, even though the Moors built on the slopes of the al-Hamma (Alfama) for five centuries (7th–12th). The remains of Moorish houses have been discovered in the grounds of the castle and there's a section of Moorish wall leading down the steps from the Miradouro de Santa Luzia to Rua Norberto de Araújo. *Tram: 12, 28. Bus: 37.*

❷ ★ Sé (Cathedral). The cathedral stands as a monument to Dom Afonso Henrique's Reconquest of Lisbon and is also the city's oldest

church. Coming uphill from the Baixa, you will be struck by the two castellated towers, framing a rosette window above the main portal. Once your eyes have adjusted to the darkness inside, you can appreciate the simple Romanesque lines and tall columns topped with a barrel-vaulted ceiling. There are Gothic side chapels, tombs, iron portals, and the double arches of the cloisters (the latter is worth paying to see). Later embellishments were removed in the 20th century to enhance the cathedral's medieval aspect. ⏲ *15–30 min. Largo da Sé.* ☎ *21-886-6752. Free admission, cloisters 2.50€. Church daily 9am–7pm; cloisters Oct–Apr only Mon–Sat 10am–6pm, Sun 2pm–6pm. Tram: 12, 28. Bus: 37.*

The cathedral is the oldest church in the city.

❸ ★★ Igreja de Santa Engrácia e Panteão Nacional. The building of this church was something of a labor of love, taking almost 300 years to complete (from 1681–1966) and giving rise to the popular expression, *Obras de Santa Engrácia* (Works of Santa Engracia) meaning something is unlikely to ever be finished. Numerous

Rossio Station is a leading example of 19th century Manueline Architecture.

architects built on João Atunes's original design to create the most complete baroque church in Portugal, with curved contours, apses, and dramatic capitals topped with bas relief. The interior is lined with intricate designs of pink and brown marble, while light filters down from the semi-circular cupola above, the height and light creating a peaceful, cool, and inspiring interior. 🕐 20–45 min. Campo de Santa Clara. 📞 21-885-4820. www.igespar.pt. Admission 3€, 50% off over 65s, 60% off student card, free under 14s, plus all on Sun and public holidays. Tues–Sun 10am–5pm. Tram: 28. Bus: 9, 25, 35, 39, 46, 81, 90, 104, 105, 107.

❹ ★ **Casa dos Bicos.** Look out for this bizarre building at the foot of the Alfama, sandwiched between run-down apartments, where lines of washing flutter between the windows. Known in English as the House of the Points or Spikes, it was built in 1523 by Dom Brás de Albuquerque (1500–80) following a trip to Italy; the texture of the walls have a striking resemblance to

Manueline Architecture

Manueline is the most elaborate form of Portuguese architecture. Spanning an approximate 50-year period from 1490 to 1540, it takes its name from Dom Manuel I, who funded construction of churches and monuments with income from the spice trade. Manueline architecture is particularly noted for its ornate, plateresque-style carvings (ornate style with its origins in Spain) with religious, regal, natural and maritime themes, as a celebration of power. Portals, windows, columns, and exterior walls display intricate stone carvings of ropes, anchors, armillary spheres (navigational instrument), coats of arms, the cross of the Order of Christ, and natural symbols such as leaves and plants. There was a resurgence of the style during the 19th century, the leading example being Rossio Station (p 65).

the diamond-shaped stones on the Palazzo dei Diamanti in the Italian city of Ferrara. The Casa dos Bicos is rarely open (except for the occasional exhibition), but the recently cleaned façade is the main feature. *Rua dos Bacalhoeiros. Tram: 18, 25. Bus: 9, 28, 35, 81, 82, 90, 746, 759, 794.*

5 ★★ **Baixa.** The neoclassical Baixa district is often referred to as the Baixa Pombalina, a reference to the Marquês de Pombal who spearheaded its construction in the 18th century (p 36). Stretching from the grand expanse of the Praça do Comércio to the Praça de Pedro IV (a.k.a. Rossio) and **Praça da Figueira** (see p 64), the easily walked grid-like structure of the Baixa represents a radical departure from the opulent palaces that stood here prior to the 1755 earthquake. As its name suggests, the new Praça do Comércio (Commerce Square) was designated for finance ministries and port authorities, with a symmetrical layout of functional buildings facing inwards, all with arched galleries on the ground floor. One side of the square was left open to the river to welcome trade while the Arco do Triunfo on the opposite side (topped with figures representing glory, valor, and genius), leads to Rua Augusta.

The buildings and streets here are simple and uniform, built for merchants and tradesmen and retaining their original names, such as silver, gold, and shoemaker streets. *Baixa Pombalina. Metro: Baixa-Chiado, Rossio. Tram: 12, 15, 28. Bus: 2, 81, 92.*

6 ★★ **Elevador de Santa Justa.** This curious iron structure caught my eye the first time I visited the Baixa. It's hard to miss, as it stands 45 meters high with steps either side leading to the Chiado. It's often called the Elevador do Carmo, as the upper level is used as access to the Convento do Carmo. It has mistakenly been attributed to Gustave Eiffel of Eiffel Tower fame but was actually designed by Porto-born architect Raul Mesnier de Ponsard. Completed in 1902, the structure is neo-Gothic with inter-level arched 'windows' topped with filigree decoration. It still functions as an elevator (and was recently overhauled), as well as a fun 'ride' for visitors. There's a cafe at the top but it's often crowded. *See p 8,* **6**.

The bizarre façade of Casa dos Bicos.

The ruins of Convento do Carmo.

7 ★★★ **Igreja do Convento do Carmo.** Only the ruins of the church remain of this once-grand 14th-century Carmelite convent, destroyed by the 1755 earthquake and the fire that followed it, but it still exudes a sense of beauty and peace. Despite having no roof, its external walls remain and the church follows a Latin-cross layout. It's a matter of filling the gaps, with help from the information boards.

Elevador de Santa Justa, which gives access to the Convento do Carmo.

There's also a small but diverse collection of archeological artifacts, including tombstones with Manueline decoration and Hebrew inscription, a decorated, stone baptismal font, and a baroque tiled panel. 🕒 *30 min–1 hr. See p 9,* **7**.

8 **Casa do Ferreiro das Tabuletas.** As you're walking around, you'll notice both functional tiles and elaborate panels decorating both the inside and outside of buildings, a practice developed since the Moorish occupation. You can learn more about this at the **Museu Nacional do Azulejo** (see p 48). On this house, find an eye-catching design dating from 1864 by Luis Ferreira (1807–70), better known as Ferreira das Tabuletas (Ferreira of the tablets or signs). *Largo Rafael Bordalo Pinheiro. Elevador da Glória.*

9 **Igreja de São Roque.** This early 16th-century church was built on the orders of the king Dom Manuel I following a devastating plague. A relic of São Roque, the protector against plagues, was brought from Venice and the church named after the saint. It was also one of the only buildings left standing after the 1755 earthquake. I like to sit a while in this peaceful church; look upwards to see the *trompe l'oeil* ceiling, large domes and paintings depicting biblical scenes. Around the edge are a series of chapels, mostly covered in gold leaf and Mannerist paintings. *The adjoining museum reopened in 2008 after a revamp and extension—here you'll find an impressive collection of religious art and objects and a model of the chapel dedicated to Saint John the Baptist.* 🕐 *15 min–1 hr. Largo da Trindade Coelho. Open Mon–Fri 8:30am–5pm, Sat & Sun 9:30am–5pm. Museum: 2.50€ adults, 1€ Lisbon Card, youth card, 5€ family. Tues-Wed, Fri–Sun 10am–6pm, Thurs 2–9pm. Elevador da Glória.*

Great War statue on Avenida da Liberdade.

🔟 **Cervejaria da Trindade** has a relaxed atmosphere, good food and walls adorned with 19th-century tiles to admire whilst you dine. At the front of the restaurant the panels reflect the romanticism of the period with images of the seasons, and at the back is a newer panel depicting the monks who once used this as their refectory. *Rua Nova da Trindade.* ☎ *21-342-3506. $$ $$$.*

⓫ ★★ **Avenida da Liberdade.** Built in the 19th century, this avenue stretches from Praça dos Restauradores to Pombal and is a symbol of modernity, modeled on the Champs Elysées in Paris. It's a pleasure to walk along here, either

The Art Deco Eden Teatro on Avenida da Liberdade.

Ornate carved arch on the Mosteiro dos Jerónimos.

on the sidewalk looking into the stores, or under the shade of the trees where you can stop for a peaceful coffee (p 61). Two of the

most iconic buildings are actually in Praça dos Restauradores: the Art Deco **Eden Teatro** (now an apart-hotel) and the imposing Palácio da Foz (now home to the tourist office). *See p 59,* ❷.

⓬ ★★★ **Mosteiro dos Jeróni-mos &** kids **Torre de Belém.**
Two of the most important examples of Manueline architecture (see box p 24), the Jeronimos Monastery and Belém Tower are UNESCO World Heritage Sites. The Tower is a compact gem of a monument with carved symbols both inside and out, while the Jeronimos Monastery is a monumental treat from its exterior portals, interior columns and vaulted ceilings to its intricate cloisters and choir. *See p 11,* ❸, *p 14,* ❽.

⓭ ★ **Pavilhão de Portugal.**
Designed for the 1998 Expo by

Torre de Belem, a World Heritage Site.

The Portugal Pavilion, designed for the 1998 Expo.

contemporary architect, Álvaro Siza Vieira, the Portugal Pavilion is a showcase of modern Lisbon. The open square in front is covered by a large concrete roof that has the appearance of a draped sheet, whilst the main entrance is located at the side of the building, aiming to keep the focus on the public spaces, rather than projecting importance on those inside. *Cais Português, Doca dos Olivais. Metro & Train: Oriente. Bus: 5, 25, 750, 759, 794.*

⓮ ★ **Estação do Oriente.** It might sound eccentric, but I love visiting Parque das Nações's train station. No, I'm not a trainspotter, this is an architectural attraction in itself. Designed by Spaniard Santiago Calatrava, the most striking feature is the platform level, a combination of metal and glass columns and roof which resembles a forest of palms. *Metro & Train: Oriente. Bus: 5, 25, 750, 759, 794.*

⓯ ★★ **Ponte de Vasco de Gama.** A fast alternative route for those heading to and from the south, this bridge keeps traffic out of the city center. Lisbon's 25 de Abril Bridge (p 35) was built during the Salazar dictatorship and was named after him until the Carnation Revolution (p 35), when it took the day's date. So while that is a reminder of the past, the Vasco da Gama Bridge represents the future—a sleek, concrete construction that snakes 12km across the tidal waters of the Tagus River. Although at the far end of the Parque das Nações, you should try and see it close up—I recommend a trip to the viewing platform of the Vasco da Gama Tower for a bird's-eye view. *Metro & Train: Oriente. Bus: 5, 25, 750, 759, 794.*

Close-up of the Ponte de Vasco de Gama bridge.

Child's Play: Lisbon with Kids

1. Oceanário
2. Pavilhão de Conhecimento
3. La Rúcula
4. Cable Car
5. Jardim Zoológico de Lisboa
6. Tagus River Boat Trip
7. Beach & Day Trips

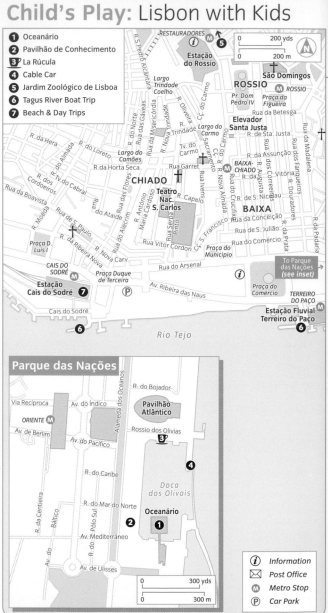

Parque das Nações

Information
Post Office
Metro Stop
Car Park

This tour guides you round some of the best child-friendly museums, attractions, and activities from Parque das Nações to the Jardim Zoológico de Lisboa or a boat trip and a day at the beach. **START: Parque das Nações. Metro: Oriente. Bus: 5, 10, 19, 21, 28, 50, 68, 81, 82, 85.**

❶ ★★★ Oceanário. An expensive but worthwhile attraction that should keep all ages happy. An easy to follow route takes you around sharks, otters, and strange underwater creatures such as sea dragons, which resemble drifting seaweed. At the end there's a shop selling cuddly sealife toys, marine-themed stationery and all kinds of books and games.🕐 1–1½ hr. Doca dos Olivais. ☎ 21-891-7002. www.oceanario.pt. Admission 12€, 6.50€ seniors, 6€ kids 4–12, free under 3s, 29€ families (2 adults/2 children under 13 yrs). Apr–Oct daily 10am–7pm, Nov–Mar daily 10am–6pm, 25 Dec 1pm–6pm, New Year's Day 12–6pm. Metro & Train: Oriente. Bus: 5, 10, 19, 21, 28, 50, 68, 81, 82, 85.

❷ ★★ Pavilhão de Conhecimento. Just a short walk from the Oceanário, the Knowledge Pavilion brims with the kind of interactive science exhibits kids enjoy. The permanent exhibits are divided into four sections appealing to children of all ages and abilities. **The Unfinished House** is for kids of 3–6 years only, and involves them helping to build a house using foam bricks whilst the **Exploratorium** looks into the science behind tornadoes to soap bubbles. Other areas include **See, Do, Learn**, and **Live Mathematics** and there are also regular temporary exhibitions. 🕐 1–1½ hr. Alameda dos Oceanos. ☎ 21-891-7100. www.pavconhecimento.pt. Admission 7€, 4€ seniors & kids 7–17, 3€ kids 3–6, free under 3s, 15€ families (1 or 2 adults with kids up to 17 years). Tues–Fri 10am–6pm, weekends & public holidays 11am–7pm. Metro & Train: Oriente. Bus: 5, 10, 19, 21, 28, 50, 68, 81, 82, 85.

❸ ★★ La Rúcula. Eating Italian is a quick and easy option to keep the whole family happy. This modern restaurant opposite the Atlantic Pavilion has oven-baked pizzas, pasta, salads, steaks, and a long list of delicious Italian desserts from tiramisu to chocolate tart, all reasonably priced. Rossio dos Olivais ☎ 21-892-2747. $$.

Eating & Entertainment

There's no shortage of eateries throughout Lisbon but shopping centers are my top choice, especially on a rainy day. The food section at such locations is a revelation—although you'll get the usual fast-food chains, there are also healthy options, sandwiches, smoothies, ice cream, and full hot meals, mostly at a good price. The city's three main shopping centers, Vasco da Gama, Colombo, and Amoreiras, also all have multi-screen movie theaters, with films often shown in English with Portuguese subtitles (always check before buying a ticket).

Parque das Nações—Getting Around

At Nations' Park there are various options to ease those tired young feet. Apart from the cable car (see below), there's a tourist mini-train that starts and finishes at Alameda dos Oceanos (by the Pavilhão Atlântico). Admission 3€, 1.75€ kids 5–12 and seniors, free under 5s. Open Jul–Sept 10am–7pm, Oct–Jun 10am–5pm.

Kids might not want to walk too far but are often keen to pedal, so try hiring bicycles and go-karts from Tejo Bike. They have two outlets here, one by the Pavilhão Atlântico, the other by Sony Park towards the bridge. Bikes can be hired from ½ an hour to 10 hours and there are many safe routes around the site. www.tejobike.pt. Bicycles 2.50€ adults, 2€ kids, go-karts 3.50€, 3€ kids, 7€ family go-kart. Mar–Oct 10am–8pm, Nov–Feb 11am–6pm.

❹ ★ **Cable Car.** Unless your kids are petrified of heights, they'll find the cable car a thrill, and it serves as a quick way to get from one end of the park to the other. Hop on the car as it passes through the station (don't worry, it's very slow), and relax as the doors close and the car rises over the buildings. Take a map and point out the different attractions, from the Oceanário and bulbous Pavilhão Atlântico to the Vasco da Gama Bridge. If you have a return, you can either jump off and return later, or stay on for a circular trip. 🕐 *10–20 min. Between Doca dos Olivais and Torre de Vasco da Gama.* ☎ *21-895-6143. www.portal dasnacoes.pt. Admission 3.90€ one way, 6€ round trip, 2€ kids 5–14 & seniors one way, 3.30€ kids 5–14 & seniors round trip, free under 5s. Oct–May Mon–Fri 11am–7pm, Sat, Sun & public holidays 10am–8pm; Jun–Sept Mon–Fri 11am–8pm, Sat, Sun & public holidays 10am–9pm. Metro & Train: Oriente. Bus: 5, 25, 28, 44, 708, 750, 759, 794.*

❺ ★★ **Jardim Zoológico de Lisboa.** Most kids love zoos and as Lisbon's is open every day of the year, it's always an option. There's everything from cheeky chimpanzees and huge hippopotami to tropical birds, reptiles, and creepy crawlies. The best parts are the feeding and demos, so try and coordinate your visit with these. 🕐 *1–3 hr. Sete Rios, Praça Marechal Humberto Delgado.* ☎ *21-723-2920. www.zoo.pt. Admission 16.50€, 13.50€ seniors, 12.50€ kids 3–11, free under 3s. Daily 10am–8pm; dolphin presentation Wed–Mon 11am & 3pm, Tues 3pm; sea lion feeding daily 10:30am*

The cable car at Parque das Nações.

Hippos at Lisbon's Zoo.

& 2pm; pelican feeding daily 2:30pm; free-flying bird demo daily 12:15pm & 4:30pm.

⑥ ★★ Tagus River Boat Trip.

During the hot summer, nothing can beat an ice cream as you glide along the river. Boat trips are a novelty and give kids an alternative view of the city from the water. It doesn't have to be expensive, as you can opt for the Transtejo river buses that run from Cais do Sodre, Terreiro do Paço, and Belém to locations on the other side. One of the best routes is to Cacilhas, from where you can take them on a bus trip to the Cristo do Rei statue (p 41). If you want more than a quick taster, take one of the tourist boats, which depart from Terreiro do Paço daily at 3pm. The trips take 2½ hours and pass various sites along the river, but you will pay quite a lot more. 🕐 *20 min–2 hr.* Fluvial stations: Cais do Sodré, Terreiro do Paço, Belém. ☎ *808-203-050.* *www.transtejo.pt. Riverbus 1.70 €, .82€ kids. Tourist boat 20€, 10€ kids & seniors. First and last (different routes vary) 5:15am–2:30am.*

⑦ ★★ Beach & Day Trips.

Fortunately from Lisbon, the beach is an easy trip to take with your kids. Trains leave regularly from Cais do Sodré to the Estoril coast, where you have several good beaches to choose from (p 148). Trains from Oriente and Entrecampos run to Sintra, which kids will relish for its fantasy palaces, Moorish castle, and toy museum (p 156).

Parque das Nações Playgrounds

Nations' Park has several specially designed play areas for kids of various ages. The Music Playground (at Passeio das Tágides, next to Garcia Horta Gardens) is an intriguing space with several bronze 'instruments' ranging from triangles and gongs to musical columns. Kids are free to jump on them to discover the different sounds that they make.

The Parque do Tejo Playground in the Tagus Gardens Park has a sandy area with wooden animals, slides, and a rope climbing frame for younger children. On the other side, the skate park attracts older kids keen to show off tricks and stunts.

The Best Special-Interest Tours

Lisbon's **Heroes**

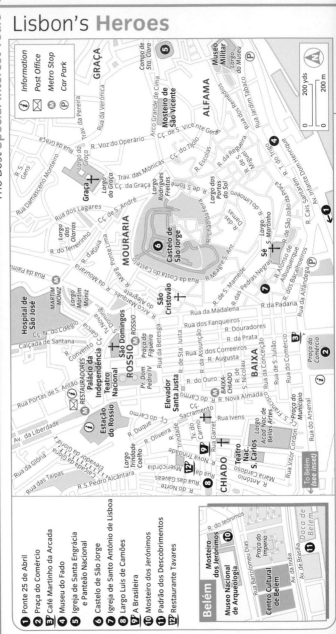

Legend:
- ℹ️ Information
- ✉️ Post Office
- Ⓜ️ Metro Stop
- 🅿️ Car Park

0 — 200 yds
0 — 200 m

Map labels include:
Campo de Sta. Clara, GRAÇA, Museu Militar, Largo do Museu, Mosteiro de São Vicente, ALFAMA, Arco Grande de Cima, Cç. de S. Vicente, R. Voz do Operário, R. do Tijolo, R. Escolas, R. da Regueira, R. de S. Miguel, R. do Trigo, R. Cais Santarém, Av. Infante Dom Henrique, Trav. das Mónicas, R. de S. Tomé, Largo Rodrigues Freitas, Largo das Portas do Sol, R. das Damas, R. de São João da Praça, R. de S. Martinho, Graça, Largo da Graça, Rua Damasceno Monteiro, Cç. da Graça, Rua dos Lagares, Cç. de S. André, Largo dos Olarias, R. do Terreirinho, R. d'Agua, R. da Mouraria, MOURARIA, Castelo de São Jorge, Recinto da Feira, R. Milagre S. Ant., Sé, Largo S. Martinho, R. Afonso de Albuquerque, R. dos Bacalhoeiros, R. da Alfândega, Rua de Palma, Largo Martim Moniz, MARTIM MONIZ, Arco Marquês de Alegrete, R. da Alegria, São Cristovão, R. de S. Mamede, R. das Pedras Negras, R. da Padaria, Hospital de São José, Cç. N. do Colégio, Calçada de Santana, T. Nova, S. Domingos, R. da Betesga, Praça da Figueira, Rua da Madalena, Rua dos Fanqueiros, R. Douradores, R. da Prata, Rua dos Correeiros, R. Augusta, Rua da Assunção, R. de S. Nicolau, Rua da Conceição, BAIXA, Rua de S. Julião, Rua do Comércio, Praça do Comércio, Convento, Palácio da Independência, RESTAURADORES, São Domingos, Teatro Nacional, ROSSIO, Pr. Dom Pedro IV, Estação do Rossio, R. de Sta. Justa, Elevador Santa Justa, R. do Carmo, R. do Ouro, R. de Sacramento, R. Nova Almada, Rua Ivens, Cç. do Sacramento, BAIXA CHIADO, Praça do Município, Rua Garrett, Largo Acad. Nac. de Bellas Artes, Teatro Nac. S. Carlos, Rua do Arsenal, Rua Portas de S. Antão, Av. da Liberdade, Calçada da Glória, Elevador da Glória, Rua das Taipas, R.S. Pedro Alcântara, R. do Norte, Rua das Gáveas, R. da Misericórdia, Largo Trindade Coelho, R. Duque, Cç. do Carmo, R. Oliveira, Tv. do Carmo, Nova Trindade, Tv. da Trindade, CHIADO, R. António Maria Cardoso, Rua Vitor Cordon, R.S. Francisco, To Belém (see inset)

Numbered points on map: ①②③④⑤⑥⑦⑨⑧⑫

---

① Ponte 25 de Abril
② Praça do Comércio
③ Café Martinho da Arcada
④ Museu do Fado
⑤ Igreja de Santa Engrácia e Panteão Nacional
⑥ Castelo de São Jorge
⑦ Igreja de Santo António de Lisboa
⑧ Largo Luís de Camões
⑨ A Brasileira
⑩ Mosteiro dos Jerónimos
⑪ Padrão dos Descobrimentos
⑫ Restaurante Tavares

Belém (inset)

⑩ Mosteiro dos Jerónimos
Museu Nacional de Arqueologia
Centro Cultural de Belém
R. de Jerónimos
Rua Bartolomeu Dias
Praça do Império
Av. da Índia
Av. de Brasília
Doca de Belém
⑪

isbon has paid tribute to the heroes who have played an important part in its unique identity. This tour gives you plenty of insight into the city's personalities, from kings and the patron saint to famous poets and singers. It gives a refreshing new slant on some of Lisbon's major attractions as well as some lesser-known corners. **START: Praça do Comércio. Metro: Baixa/Chiado. Tram: 12, 15. Bus: 2, 81, 92, 711, 713.**

1 ★ Ponte 25 de Abril. This striking red suspension bridge runs from Lisbon to Almada, where the Cristo Rei statue stands, arms wide. When it was inaugurated in 1966, it was named after the dictator, Salazar, who led the right-wing *Estado Novo* (new state) here for 36 years. It was renamed after the date of the Carnation Revolution, when the dictatorship was brought to a peaceful end in a bloodless, left-wing coup, led by the military. On 25th April, 1974 they came out onto the streets, joined by thousands of the general public who brought carnations from the market. The bridge pays homage to all the heroes of the revolution and the Portuguese people who brought

Dom Jose I, king at the time of the 1755 earthquake

The 200-year-old Café Martinho da Arcada.

democracy to the country. ⏱ *20 min. Train: Alcântara. Tram: 15. Bus: 27, 28, 29, 43, 49, 51, 112..*

2 ★★ Praça do Comércio. The center of the recently renovated square is dominated by a bronze of Dom Jose I (king from 1750–77), commissioned by Pombal (see box below) as a homage to the king for rebuilding the city after the earthquake of 1755. It was Pombal who took control of the reconstruction, creating this airy neo-classical square surrounded by arches and the grid-like Baixa north of it. As well as the statue itself, make sure you also look at the pedestal—determined to be remembered; Pombal inserted a bronze medallion of himself as the real force behind the new direction for the city. *See p 7,* **1**.

3 Café Martinho da Arcada. This 200-year-old cafe and restaurant exudes 19th-century Portuguese elegance—rich dark wood, tiles and mirrors, and the aroma of fresh coffee and cakes beckoning from the counter. Fernando Pessoa (see below) was a regular and there is a corner dedicated to him in the restaurant. *Praça de Comércio, 3.* ☎ *21-887-9259. $$$.*

4 ★★ **Museu do Fado.** As a museum and cultural center, this is the key place for learning more about all aspects of fado, Portugal's haunting and very distinctive genre of melancholy folk song. Located at the foot of the Alfama, this permanent exhibition explores the development from the 19th century to the present with a display of Portuguese guitars and a prized collection of brochures, posters, and photos. Look out for pieces on such stars as Maria Severa, Maria do Carmo, and guitarist Carlos Paredes as well as Amália Rodrigues (see box), alongside contemporary singers such as Mariza. ⏲ *30–45 min. Largo do Chafariz.* ☎ *21-882-3470. Admission 3€, 1.50€ kids*

Dom Afonso Henriques, Portugal's first king.

4–18 years & students with ID, 1.75€ Lisboa Card. Tues–Sat 10am–6pm. Bus: 9, 28, 35, 81, 82.

5 ★★ **Igreja de Santa Engrácia e Panteão Nacional.** The tombs and cenotaphs inside the National Pantheon read like a who's who of Lisbon's (and Portugal's) history. It's not macabre though; this is a masterpiece of Portuguese baroque architecture—the marble interiors serving as a cool retreat from the hot Lisbon sun, and the roof, a tranquil place to spy on the city. The church's central area (in the shape of a Greek cross) includes cenotaphs dedicated to writer Luís de Camões (c.1524–80) and explorer Vasco da Gama (1460–1524), and four corner

Three Heroes

Born in Lisbon as Sebastião José Cavalho e Melo, Marquês de **Pombal** (1699–1782) was prime minister from 1750–77. He is most remembered in Lisbon for spearheading the rebuilding of the city after the earthquake, replacing the luxurious waterfront palaces with the neoclassical Baixa, built for the merchant classes and tradesmen.

Fernando Pessoa (1888–1935) became part of the vanguard of modern literature, meeting with other writers in Café Martinho da Arcada and A Brasileira, and is most renowned for writing under heteronyms. The most famous of these are Ricardo Reis and Bernardo Soares, and his best works are considered to be *The Book of Disquiet* and *Message*.

Amália Rodrigues (1920–99) helped shape modern fado music and many of her recordings are used as standards for the genre. She first sang professionally in 1939 and appeared in movies such as *Capas Negras* (1947). She released her final album, *Segredo,* two years before she died.

rooms house the tombs of former presidents, writers, and other personalities. The most touching is that of fado singer Amália Rodrigues, the only woman entombed at the pantheon, which is often laden with fresh flowers. ⏱ *20–45 min. Campo de Santa Clara.* ☎ *21-885-4820. Admission 2.50€, 1.25€ over 65s, 1€ student card, free under 15s, plus all on Sun and public holidays. Tues–Sun 10am–5pm. Tram: 28. Bus: 12, 34.*

6 ★★★ Castelo de São Jorge. Of course Lisbon's castle is a mustsee on any trip to the city and when there, seek out the statue of Dom Afonso Henriques (1109–85) in the Praça das Armas, the large, cool and leafy square just through the turnstiles that offers breathtaking views across the city. Portugal's first king, he drove the Moors out of the city in 1147. Dressed in mail armor, his sword raised and his shield bearing a cross, he appears powerful and strong, a crusading king who led his men from the front and now stands surveying his prize. See p 8, **4**.

7 ★ Igreja de Santo António de Lisboa. This church is dedicated to St Anthony (1195–1231), the patron saint of Lisbon. Located

St Anthony, patron saint of Lisbon.

in a tree-lined square close to the cathedral, on the site of the house where the saint's parents lived. Not much remains of the original church but the reconstruction is simple and attractive with white, pink, and yellow marble inlays. The square, with a typical statue of St Anthony holding a child comes alive during the week before and after the St Anthony's Day celebrations on 13th

Castelo de São Jorge.

Vasco da Gama & Luís Vaz de Camões

Vasco da Gama (c. 1460–1524) is one of the most notable figures in Portugal's Golden Age of Discovery. He established a sea route to India, making all the seafaring 'discoveries' of his predecessors worthwhile, as there was now no need for goods to be brought via the arduous Silk Road through the Middle East.

Luís Vaz de Camões (c.1524–80), born in Lisbon, is also connected with the discoveries, but through writing. Living a life on the edge, he took part in military expeditions, lost his right eye in Ceuta, bedded many a court lady, and was sent to Goa after injuring a member of the Royal Stables. He wrote his most famous work, *Os Lusiadas* (The Lusiads), while in Macau, an epic poem that charts Por- tuguese history, focusing on Vasco da Gama's trip to India.

Luis Vas de Camões tomb inside Jeronimos Monastery.

June, when the area buzzes with impromptu bars, fado music, grilled sardines, and plenty of wine.

🕐 *10–15 min. Largo de Santo António da Sé.* ☎ *21-886-9145. Free admission. Daily 8am–7:30pm. Tram: 12, 28. Bus: 37.*

8 ★ **Largo Luis de Camões.** At the juncture between the Chiado and the Bairro Alto proper, this is really a passing-through point, with tram-stops, shops, and cafes on either side. At its center is a statue of Luis de Camões (see box, above), Portugal's most renowned writer, after whom the square is named. *Metro: Baixa-Chiado. Bairro Alto. Tram: 28. Bus: 58, 92, 790.*

Detail of stained glass window, Mosteiro dos Jerónimos.

Padrão dos Descobrimentos with Henry the Navigator at the bow.

9 ★★ **A Brasileira.** This cafe is among the best known in Lisbon and located on a well-trodden tourist route. Crowds of people hang round to see the striking bronze statue of Fernando Pessoa seated outside the cafe. It's a pleasant place to sit in the summer months and contemplate the lives of struggling writers in 1920s' Lisbon. *Rua Garrett 100–122.* ☎ *21-346-9541. $–$$*

10 ★★★ **Mosteiro dos Jerónimos.** Take tram 15 to Belém to see one of the most celebrated monuments in the city. As an example of Manueline architecture this (along with the Torre de Belém by the river, p 14) is one of the most prized examples. As you enter the main portal, you'll see two elaborate tombs. On the left is Fernando Pessoa and on the right the explorer Vasco da Gama. In the summer it can get overrun with noisy tours and flashing cameras, so if you want to find peace in the church and the space to examine the elaborate décor, come in low season. *See p 11,* **3**.

11 ★★★ **Padrão dos Descobrimentos.** The Discoveries Monument is one of the most iconic monuments in Lisbon. Towering more than 50 meters high and located on the edge of the Tagus River, it was built in 1960 for the 500th anniversary of the death of Henry the Navigator and as a homage to those that took part in the Golden Age of Discovery. It takes the form of a *caravela*, the ships used by Portuguese seafarers and on the bow stand Henry the Navigator, Vasco da Gama, Pedro Alvares Cabral, Ferdinand Magellan, Diogo Cão, Afonso de Albuquerque, Luís de Camões, and Dom Manuel I, among others. There's seating around the sculpture, a good place to rest before heading back into the city center. *See p 15,* **9**.

12 **Restaurante Tavares.** Tavares is Lisbon's oldest restaurant and famed for having once been a hangout of renowned writers such as Eça de Queiros. Not a cheap restaurant by Portuguese standards, but worth a visit for the palatial interiors and quality gastronomy that has now earned a Michelin star. *R da Misericordia.* ☎ *21-342-1112. $$$$$.*

True Romance

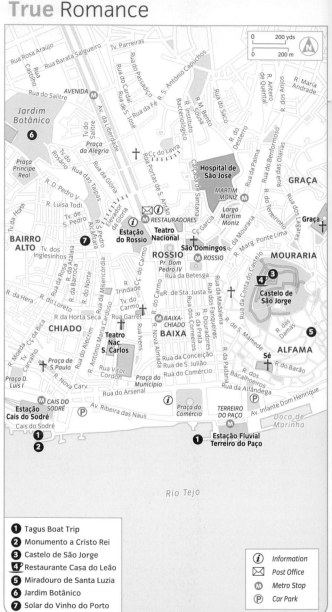

1. Tagus Boat Trip
2. Monumento a Cristo Rei
3. Castelo de São Jorge
4. Restaurante Casa do Leão
5. Miradouro de Santa Luzia
6. Jardim Botânico
7. Solar do Vinho do Porto

i	Information
✉	Post Office
Ⓜ	Metro Stop
Ⓟ	Car Park

Lisbon has plenty of places for strolling, escaping from the crowds, and cozy restaurants. On this tour you will encounter classic vantage points, offering plenty of scope for sharing moments to savor the seductive qualities of the city, from the shade of the Jardim Botânico to a quiet drink in the Solar. START: **Terreiro do Paço fluvial station. Tram: 15, 18, 25. Bus: 2, 81, 92, 711, 713. Cais do Sodré fluvial station. Tram: 15, 18, 25. Bus: 6, 35, 36, 40, 44, 45, 58, 82, 91.**

Castelo de São Jorge crowns the ancient Alfama district.

1 ★★ kids **Tagus Boat Trip.** Whatever time of year, you can snuggle up together on one of Transtejo's tourist boats along the Tagus river, leaving from the Fluvial station at Terreiro do Paço daily at 3pm. Alternatively, if you're going to the Cristo Rei (see below) you can hop on a river bus, a relatively quick and much cheaper option. *See p 33,* **6**.

2 ★★ kids **Monumento a Cristo Rei.** One of the city's great landmarks, the Statue of Christ the King is actually in Almada on the south side of the Tagus. Either take an organized bus tour or hop on a river bus from Cais do Sodré to Cacilhas and then take bus no.101 (approximately every 20 min) from outside the fluvial station to the Cristo

Monumenta a Cristo Rei.

Stop at a viewing point on your way down from the castle.

Rei front gates. Buy a ticket and take the elevator to the top of the statue. Around 110 meters high, it is based on the statue that looks down from Corcovado mountain over Rio de Janeiro in Brazil. Once out of the elevator, climb a few more steps to the very top—it can get windy up here, so hold onto each other for good measure. It's good to get here at the latest by mid-morning so you can get back to Lisbon for lunch. On a clear summer's day, the sun is behind the statue in late morning so you have superb views and good light for photos of the 25 de Abril Bridge below and the Lisbon panorama beyond. What's more, when the sun is directly behind the head of the statue, it appears like a glowing halo. ⏱ *30 min–1 hr. plus 45 min return trip by ferry and bus. Alto de Pragal, Almada.* ☎ *21-275-1000. www.cristorei.pt. Admission 4€, 2€ under 8s. Winter daily 9:30am–6:15pm, summer Mon–Fri 9:30am–6:30pm, Sat–Sun 9:30am–7pm. Bus: 101 from Cacilhas.*

❸ ★★★ **Castelo de São Jorge.** One of Lisbon's most notable attractions, perched on top of the Alfama hill, St George's Castle is mostly a modern reconstruction (p 8 and p 53), which some find reason to criticize. But immerse yourself in thoughts of where you are, think about the fact that it lies at the ancient heart of Lisbon, from where Romans, Moors, and Portuguese kings guarded their city for centuries, and you'll discover the romance of this place—much of it unchanged through centuries. Head up here after lunch, when most of the tourist coaches have dashed off elsewhere. Or come here for lunch (see below) and then wander through the shade of the Praça das Armas, climb the turrets for ever-better views, and wander back through the cobbled streets of Santa Cruz, the district within the castle walls, with white-washed houses and small souvenir shops that give it a village feel. *See p 8,* ❹.

☕ Located inside St George's Castle, the **Restaurante Casa do Leão** has carefully incorporated the vaulted brick ceiling of the former palace with a tiled bar and elegant figures on the wall. Book a table for a romantic meal of Portuguese or international cuisine, from local bacalhau to juicy steaks. *Castelo de São Jorge.* ☎ *21-888-0154. $$$$.*

❺ ★ Miradouro de Santa Luzia. Stroll back down from the castle and stop at this viewing point to peek through the port-holes in the white wall, which frame the river like a landscape painting. At either end of the wall are a small church run by the Order of Malta and large tiled panel of the city, while to the left (as you face the river) the Portas do Sol viewing point opens out onto a bright esplanade where you can stop for coffee. Walk back downhill to the Baixa, where you can board a metro to Rato. *See p 8, ❸*.

❻ ★★ Jardim Botânico. Tucked away behind the Museu Nacional de História Nacional, the Botanic Garden is a city oasis. Afternoons are very pleasant here; tall tropical trees rise above your head, and the sun trickles through the leaves. A warren of mosaic pathways and steps, palms and magnolia trees, you can sit on a bench by a pond of water lilies and only just be aware of the distant hum of the traffic. ⏱ *45 min–2 hr. Rua da Escola Politécnica, 58.* ☎ *21-392-1800. www. jb.ul.pt. Admission 1.50€, .75€ seniors, students, youth card holders, free under 6s. Apr–Oct Mon–Fri 9am–8pm, Sat & Sun 10am–8pm; Nov–Mar Mon–Fri 9am–6pm, Sat & Sun 10am–6pm. Metro: Rato. Bus: 58 (stops outside entrance), 92, 711, 790.*

❼ Solar do Vinho do Porto. Occupying a former palace with low lights and stone walls, the deep sofas provide instant relief to those aching feet. Select a quiet corner, choose from the menu of ports and accompany it with a few savory nibbles. *Rua de São Pedro de Alcântara, 45.* ☎ *21-347-5707. www.ivp. pt. Open Mon–Sat 11am–Midnight.*

Explore the Jardim Botanico's intimate butterfly house.

The Best Special-Interest Tours

Art Club

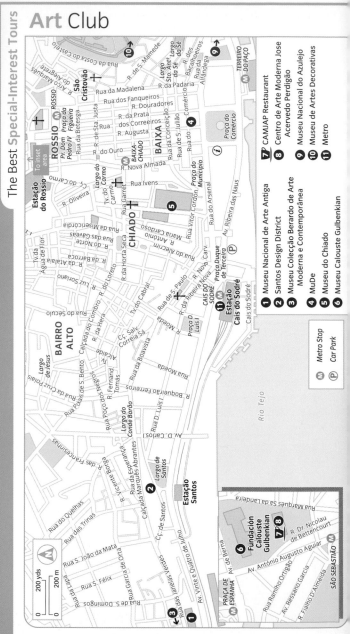

1. Museu Nacional de Arte Antiga
2. Santos Design District
3. Museu Colecção Berardo de Arte Moderna e Contemporânea
4. MuDe
5. Museu do Chiado
6. Museu Calouste Gulbenkian
7. CAMJAP Restaurant
8. Centro de Arte Moderna Jose Acervedo Perdigão
9. Museu Nacional do Azulejo
10. Museu de Artes Decorativas
11. Metro

Ⓜ Metro Stop
Ⓟ Car Park

This tour takes in the best of Lisbon's art collections, but some of them are so vast you'll probably want to spread it over a couple of days. There's everything from ancient religious painting from the Middle Ages and decorative art from the Far East to contemporary Portuguese installations. START: **Museu Nacional de Arte Antiga. Tram: 15, 28. Bus: 6, 28, 60, 713, 714, 727, 794.**

1 ★★★ Museu Nacional de Arte Antiga. You need at least an hour to see the National Museum of Ancient Art's highlights, more if you want to appreciate it fully. It's considered the most important museum in the country for both the value and chronological breadth of its collection. There are vast groups of work dating from the 8th–19th centuries, so you'll need to be selective. The large vibrant paintings of St Vincent attributed to Portuguese Renaissance artist Nuno Gonçalves (active 1450–71) are particularly outstanding, along with the 13th- and 14th-century Portuguese sculptures in wood and gilt, and the Dutch still life works. The Art of the Portuguese Expansion includes everything from elaborate

Building façades in Santas Design District.

hand-painted screens from China to Indian furniture and African masks. See p 10, **1**.

Museu Nacional de Arte Antiga.

Museu Colecção Berardo de Arte Moderna e Contemporânea.

❷ ★ Santos Design District.

Santos is the area between the MNAA and the Mercado da Ribeira in Praça Dom Luis spread along the riverfront inland a few blocks. Once an industrial area, it is now a trendy place to explore and an avant-garde design district. Santos also has its fair share of museums, including MNAA, Museu das Comunicações, and Museu da Marioneta. *Tram: 15, 28. Bus: 6, 28, 60, 714, 732.*.

❸ ★★ Museu Colecção Berardo de Arte Moderna e Contemporânea.

In 2007, the Berardo Collection of Contemporary and Modern Art opened at the Belém Cultural Center (CCB). At first I was sorry that the CCB had ended its era of hosting top-notch, temporary exhibitions and

being home to the Design Museum (see above), but on visiting the Berardo Collection, it was apparent it was offering a comprehensive, developing overview of modern and contemporary art—and it's free (at the time of writing). The museum displays a collection of more than 860 pieces (and rising) by rotation, according to artistic movement from the 20th century to the present. You can expect works by Pablo Picasso, Salvador Dalí, Marcel Duchamp, Francis Bacon, Max Ernst, and plenty of rising stars. Either drop in or check out their program in advance to see what's on display. ⏱ *1 hr–1½ hr. Praça do Imperio.* ☎ *21-361-2400. www.museu berardo.com. Free*

Chinese porcelain on display at Museu Calouste Gulbenkian.

admission at time of writing, but phone for latest charges. Daily 10am–6pm (Fri until 10pm). Tours in English, 4pm Sat. Train: Belém. Tram: 15. Bus: 27, 28, 29, 43, 49, 51, 112.

④ ★★ **MuDe.** Lisbon's former Design Museum has reopened as a superb new Museum of Design and Fashion or MuDe (*mude* means 'change' in Portuguese) in the heart of the Baixa. When I visited the museum, four hardboard figures of the Beatles towered outside, an invitation to visit the Sixties exhibition inside. Housed in the shell of a former bank, the building is little more than a shell but the rough, concrete walls and stripped ceilings provide a derelict chic appearance for the museum's vintage couture and design collection. Arranged chronologically, it includes pieces by luminaries such as Coco Chanel, Givenchy, and Frank O. Gehry. The temporary displays are held upstairs and explore specific periods in more detail ⏱ *45 min–1 hr. Rua Augusta, 24. ☎ 21 000 6117. www.mude.pt. Free admission. Daily 10am–6pm (Fri until 10pm). Metro: Baixa Chiado. Tram: 12, 15, 25, 28.*

Museu do Chiado.

⑤ ★ **Museu do Chiado.** If you like the Modernists this is the place to see painting and architecture in Lisbon. First opened in 1911, it gained a new home in 1994 following the Chiado fire eight years earlier. The neo-modern building's airy reception is inviting and you can enjoy the collection at your leisure, surrounded by the unusual bluish light that reflects from the Cascais

Museu Calouste Gulbenkian.

stone floors. Lack of space means the museum presents its collection on constant rotation. So you're as likely to see a retrospective of 19th-century Portuguese art as you are works from the 1990s and contemporary period. ⏲ *45 min–1 hr. Rua Serpa Pinto 4.* ☎ *21-343-2148. www.museudochiado-ipmuseus.pt. Admission 4€, 50% discount 15–25 years & seniors, 60% youth card holders, free under 14s & Lisboa Card. Open Tues–Sun 10am–6pm. Metro: Baixa-Chiado. Tram: 28. Bus: 58, 100.*

6 ★★★ **Museu Calouste Gulbenkian.** Owing its existence to collector and benefactor Calouste Sarkis Gulbenkian (p 16), this museum appeals to wide tastes, with a little of everything from Egyptian sculpture and Oriental decorative arts to fine European paintings. Amongst the treasures is a superb collection of Islamic Art, comprising hand-painted ceramics with geometric designs, glazed tiles, prayer niches, and mosque lamps with engraved passages from the Qur'an. The Persian silks and an Armenian bible, with painted illustrations inlaid with gilt, are also noteworthy. Amongst the European art you'll find everything from an elaborate 14th-century carved diptych of the Passion of Christ to the French sculptor August Rodin's *Jean D'Aire, Burgher of Calais,* plus a fine selection of paintings by Rousseau, Manet, Degas, Renoir, and Monet. *See p 16,* **1**.

7 **CAMJAP Restaurant.** Not only is this a convenient stop-off when you're visiting several museums, but you can get a good hot meal here for around 6.50€. There's a self-service buffet, or you can just have a coffee and enjoy the view over the CAMJAP museum garden. *Rua Madre de Deus.* ☎ *21-810-0340. Open Tues–Sun during museum hours.$–$$.*

8 ★★★ **Centro de Arte Moderna Jose Acervedo Perdigão.** Part of the Calouste Gulbenkian Foundation is in a modern building designed by José Sommer Ribeiro. Opened in 1983, it has landscaped gardens which provide an ideal setting for outdoor sculpture and the museum gives a fine overview of Portuguese and international art from 1910 onwards. Look out for works by Sonia and Robert Delaunay, Maria Helena Vieira da Silva, Arpad

Centro Arte Moderna Jose Acervedo Perdigão.

Art on the underground.

Szenes, and Cândido Portinari. I was also impressed by the collection of works by British artists such as Antony Gormley, and an Armenian collection, including paintings by Arshile Gorky. ⏲ *1 hr–1½ hr. Rua Dr Nicolau Bettencourt.* ☎ *21-823-474. www. camjap.gulbenkian.pt. Admission 2€, combined Gulbenkian & CAMJAP 5€, free seniors & students & Sun. Open Tues–Sun 10am–6pm. Metro: São Sebastião, Praça de Espanha. Bus: 16, 26, 31, 46, 56.*

⑨ ★★★ Museu Nacional do Azulejo. The National Tile Museum chronologically follows the development of techniques used to make *azulejos*. Following the changes within the tile industry, you also begin to understand social, cultural, economic, and political history. My top picks include the early imitations of Moorish tiles featuring knots and twists; 16th-century panels influenced by the Renaissance styles from Flanders, particularly the *Painel de Nossa Senhora da Vida*; an elaborate religious scene by Marçal de Matos, c. 1580, depicting the Virgin and other figures; and from the 'Cycle of the Masters,' a panel by Willem van der Kloet (1666–1747), which shows aristocrats dancing on a terrace. In the 20th century, António Costa's Art Deco

tiles stand out for their artistic finesse, but for the best modern tiles, take a look in the metro (see ⑪). ⏲ *1 hr–1½ hr. Rua Madre de Deus.* ☎ *21-810-0340. mnazulejo. imc-ip.pt. Admission 4€, 2€ 15–25 years, seniors, teachers, 1.60€ youth card holders, free under 15s, Sun & bank hols until 2pm, Lisbon Card holders Tues 2pm–6pm, Wed– Sun 10am–6pm, closed Mon, Easter Sun, New Year, 1 May, 25 Dec. Bus: 718, 742, 794 (stop outside the*

Cherub at the Museu Nacional dos Azulejos.

Museu de Artes Decorativas.

museum), 25, 759 (Avenida Dom Henrique).

⑩ ★ Museu de Artes Decorativas. This decorative arts museum is set in an eye-catching Alfama palace dating back to the 17th century. Inside, it's like stepping back into an 18th-century aristocrat's home, with a large collection of period furniture, textiles, tiles, porcelain, and glassware. The added bonus of this museum is that it runs courses teaching traditional crafts. ⊕ *45 min–1 hr. Largo das Portas do Sol, 2. ☎ 21-888-1991. www.fress.pt. Admission 4€, 2€ seniors/students, 3.20€ Lisboa Card, free under 12s. Thurs–Sun 10am–5pm.*

⑪ Metro. Lisbon's metro is the best place to see modern azulejos, and you can do it while on the move. My top five include: **Alto dos Moinhos** station with images of Fernando Pessoa by Julio Pomar; **Campo Grande,** a pastiche on 17th-century tiles placed in the wrong order by Eduardo Nery; the library images by Bartolomeu Cid dos Santos in **Entre Campos** station; the paintings of fruit at **Laranjeiras;** and the brightly colored abstract scenes by Yayoi-Kusama at **Oriente** (also see the contemporary panels throughout the Parque das Nações, see p 18). *Open daily 6:30am–1am.* ●

The **Alfama**

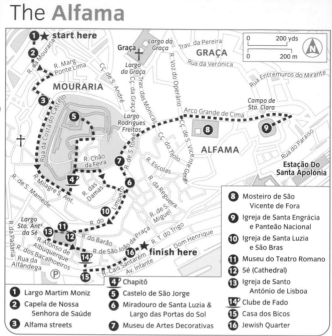

- ❶ Largo Martim Moniz
- ❷ Capela de Nossa Senhora de Saúde
- ❸ Alfama streets
- ❹ Chapitô
- ❺ Castelo de São Jorge
- ❻ Miradouro de Santa Luzia & Largo das Portas do Sol
- ❼ Museu de Artes Decorativas
- ❽ Mosteiro de São Vicente de Fora
- ❾ Igreja de Santa Engrácia e Panteão Nacional
- ❿ Igreja de Santa Luzia e São Bras
- ⓫ Museu do Teatro Romano
- ⓬ Sé (Cathedral)
- ⓭ Igreja de Santo António de Lisboa
- ⓮ Clube de Fado
- ⓯ Casa dos Bicos
- ⓰ Jewish Quarter

The hilly Alfama is the birthplace of the city, an ancient and crumbling neighborhood in parts, but one with a strong character and sense of community. On the way up to the castle and back down to the Baixa you'll absorb a good helping of daily life, maybe discovering a fashionable terrace bar or *fado* restaurant, and spotting the decorative *azulejos* (tiles) on old buildings. **START: Metro: Martim Moniz.**

❶ **Largo Martim Moniz.** Exit from the metro onto this large, redeveloped square. Situated between the Baixa and Mouraria, this is a good place to start the walk as you have the option of avoiding the steep climb upwards. If you don't fancy the first part of the walk you can take tram 28 from here and jump off at the Museu de Artes Decorativas (p 50) and pick up the walk from there.

❷ ★ **Capela de Nossa Senhora de Saúde.** This small chapel is between the left-hand side of the square (as you look towards Hotel Mundial) and Rua da Mouraria. It's dedicated to the 'Virgin of Health' for having put an end to a plague in 1569. Admire the elaborate wood and gold leaf altar, and the intricate panels of tiles lining the walls. ⏱ *10 min. Mon–Fri 8:45am–6pm; Sat 8:45am–1pm & 3–6pm; Sun & public holidays 8:45am–Noon.*

3 ★ **Alfama streets.** On the same side of the square is a steep set of steps, Escadinhas da Saúde. Brace your muscles and climb them to the top. Then turn right onto Rua Marquês Ponte de Lima (don't be surprised if local women lean out of the windows above to chat across the street with a neighbor) and then left (a few more steps) and right onto Costa do Castelo. A typical cobbled Alfama street, here you'll see various examples of functional tiles on the outside of the houses. Some of the houses in this area have been here for generations, the tiles added later. Mass produced, rather than artistic, the tiles help keep the weather out, and are seen as key features of the city's streetscape. Look out for the tiles on the right with country scenes along the top, and at a bend in the road a fine residential property displaying blue and white tiles with religious iconography.

4 ★ **Chapitô.** This trendy arts center has two terraces, perfect for alfresco lunches in the shade, as well as indoor seating. Choose from soup and toasted sandwiches or queue up with the locals for the daily Portuguese special. *Costa do Castelo, 1/7* ☎ *218-867-334 www. chapito.org. $$.*

5 ★★★ **Castelo de São Jorge.** After Chapitô the road becomes Rua do Milagre de Santo António, and you'll see the first of several tourist shops. Turn left into Rua Bartolomeu de Gusmão and walk to the top. Enter the castle precincts through the **Arco de São Jorge** (Arch of St George), which along with the castle walls marks the ancient perimeter of the fortress. The path bears right into Rua de Santa Cruz do Castelo. Santa Cruz is a small community living on a few streets within the castle walls. Other sites within the castle walls include the Casa do Governador (ticket office and shop) and, past the ticket barrier, the **Praça das Armas** (large square and viewing point), the **Royal Palace** (now home to the castle café and Casa do Leão restaurant), the Castelejo (castle towers and internal walls), and the Islamic

Decorated streets by the castle.

View over the city from Castelo de São Jorge.

Quarter. This is now known as the Praça Nova or New Square and archeological digs have revealed remains of several 11th- and 12th-century houses.

From outside the castle cafe you can spy the Solar do Castelo Heritage Hotel (see p 145) through the fence opposite. Located on Rua das Cozinhas, the palace kitchens are believed to have been here. *See p 8,* ④.

⑥ ★★ **Miradouro de Santa Luzia & Largo das Portas do Sol.** As you exit the castle grounds, follow the wall to the left along the cobbled street round to the right by the Belmonte Hotel (see p 144) and head downhill until you come to the tram tracks and the Miradouro de Santa Luzia. This viewing point is by the **Igreja de Santa Luzia** (see ⑩). Note the steps on the right of the patio (Rua Norberto de Araujo) date back to the Moorish occupation. Looking towards the hill on the left, the large white building with two bell towers is the **Mosteiro de São Vicente de Fora** (monastery and church). *See p 55,* ⑧.

⑦ ★ **Museu de Artes Decorativas (Museum of Decorative Arts).** Housed in the 17th-century Azurara Palace, this array of period

Glossary

avenida avenue
azulejos tiles
capela chapel
casa house
castelo castle
fado a type of melancholy Portuguese folk song
igreja church
jardim garden
miradouro viewpoint

mosteiro monastery
museu museum
parque park
praça square
rio river
rua street
sé cathedral
teatro theater
torre tower

furniture, textiles, tiles, porcelain, and glassware offers an insight into the trappings of aristocratic life during the 18th century. The collection was brought together by Ricardo do Espirito Santo in the mid-20th century, and donated by him to the state. A foundation in his name runs workshops and courses here in traditional crafts. Hop on tram 28 heading towards Graça or follow the tram tracks, which zigzag along the narrow Alfama streets. *See p 50,* ⑩.

⑧ ★★ Mosteiro de São Vicente de Fora.

The tram stops right outside this monastery. It's worth paying the entrance fee to enter this hidden gem (through the gates on the right), to see the impressive tile-paneled cloisters, sacristy with intricate polychrome marble inlays, and the tombs of two Teutonic knights who helped Dom Afonso Henriques during the *Reconquista* (Christian reconquest) of 1147. You can also enjoy views of the Alfama, Tagus, and Cristo Rei from the bell tower. On the ground floor there is a peaceful courtyard cafe with seating under the trellises. ⏲ *45 min–1 hr. Largo de São Vicente.* ☎ *218-824-400. Monastery admission 4€ adults. Open Mon–Sat 9am–12:30pm; Sun 3–5pm.*

⑨ ★★ Igreja de Santa Engrácia e Panteão Nacional.

Located behind the church and monastery, the Church of St Engrácia was designated the National Pantheon in 1916 and houses the tombs of several Lisbon heroes, but it's also a cool retreat from the hot Lisbon sun. Large and airy, the interior is inlaid with marble and you can go up into the dome and contemplate the colors of the city beneath. Go shortly before the church closes and you might have it to yourself. *See p 23,* ③.

⑩ ★ Igreja de Santa Luzia e São Bras.

This church is dedicated to Santa Luzia, from which the nearby Miradouro de Santa Luzia (see p 8) takes its name. It was built in the 12th century and funded by Dom Afonso Henriques as a reward for the Order's help in reconquering

Mosteiro de São Vicente de Fora has impressive interior decoration.

the city. In 1988, a fire damaged a good part of the church including the elaborately painted ceiling. You can just about see the remaining part in the sacristy; the rest of the church has been renovated. In front of the church is a small viewing area with 'port-holes' in the wall looking down towards the river. ⏱ *10–20 min. Largo de Santa Luzia.* ☎ *21-888-1303. Admission donations.*

⑪ ★ Museu do Teatro Romano. This small museum (on the right before the Sé) is on the site of a Roman theater abandoned in the 4th century and hidden from view until the late 18th century. You can view the archeological finds and see through multimedia displays what it would have been like originally. ⏱ *30 min. Pátio de Aljube, 5 (off Rua Augusta Rosa).* ☎ *21-751-3200. www.museuteatroromano.pt.*

Free admission. Tues–Sun 10am–1pm and 2–6pm.

⑫ ★ Sé (Cathedral). Lisbon's Cathedral is not the religious centerpiece of the city (this is actually the Mosteiro dos Jerónimos, see p 11). This 12th-century Romanesque church has a simple but impressive façade framed by two towers, a vaulted ceiling, a stained glass window of St Anthony, cloisters, and a 14th-century ambulatory chapel and apse. *See p 8,* ❺.

⑬ ★ Igreja de Santo António de Lisboa. Dedicated in medieval times to St Anthony, the patron saint of Lisbon, this church was rebuilt after the 1755 earthquake and displays a mixture of architectural styles. Highlights are the baroque portal, the rococo panel on the south façade, and the barrel-vaulted marble ceiling. *See p 37,* ❼.

Lisbon's 12th Century Cathedral.

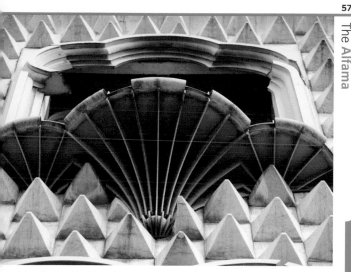

The spiky façade of Casa dos Bicos.

14 ★★★ **Clube de Fado.** Just round the corner from the Sé, this is a renowned fado restaurant and a good place to hear live music in the heart of the Alfama. Book ahead, as it's a popular venue, where owner and fado guitarist Mario Pacheco often performs. *Rua São João da Praça, 94. www.clube-de-fado.com. $$$$.*

15 ★ **Casa dos Bicos.** Walk through to Rua dos Bacalhoeiros to see the curious House of Points. It's rarely open to the public, but worth seeing for its spiky façade. Built in 1523 by Dom Brás de Albuquerque, it's believed he was influenced by buildings seen on a trip to Italy. *See p 24, ❹.*

16 ★ **Jewish Quarter.** Jews were an important part of the community prior to the Reconquest and small enclaves continued to exist until the *autos da fé* (executions) started in Rossio Square in the 16th century. They lived at the foot of the Alfama

in the poor narrow streets, sandwiched between Rua dos Cais de Santarém and Rua de São Pedro. 🕐 *20 min. Metro: Baixa-Chiado. Tram: 15, 18, 25. Bus: 2, 81, 92, 711, 713.*

Alfama Tiles.

Avenida-Parque

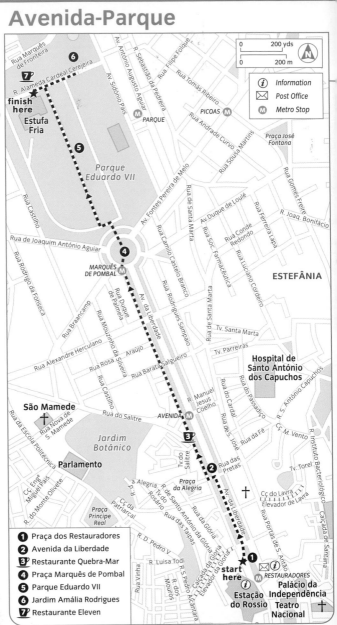

0	200 yds
0	200 m

(i) Information
✉ Post Office
Ⓜ Metro Stop

Rua Marquês de Fronteira

6

7 finish here
R. Alameda Cardeal Cerejeira

Estufa Fria

R. António Augusto Aguiar

Av. Sidónio Pais

R. Sebastião da Pedreira

Rua Filipe Folque

Rua Tomás Ribeiro

PICOAS Ⓜ

Rua Andrade Curvo

PARQUE Ⓜ

Praça José Fontana

Rua Sousa Martins

Rua Gomes Freire

R. Joaq. Bonifácio

5

Parque Eduardo VII

Av. Fontes Pereira de Melo

Rua de Santa Marta

Av. Duque de Loulé

Rua Camilo Castelo Branco

Rua Soc. Farmacêutica

Rua Conde Redondo

Rua Ferreira Lapa

Rua Luciano Cordeiro

ESTEFÂNIA

Rua Castilho

Rua de Joaquim António Aguiar

4

MARQUÊS DE POMBAL Ⓜ

Rua Rodrigo da Fonseca

Rua Braancamp

Rua Duque de Palmela

Av. da Liberdade

Rua Rodrigues Sampaio

Rua de Santa Marta

Tv. Santa Marta

Hospital de Santo António dos Capuchos

Rua Alexandre Herculano

Rua Mouzinho da Silveira

Araújo

Rua Rosa Silveira

Rua Barata Salgueiro

Tv. Parreiras

Rua do Cardal

R. S. António Capuchos

R. Instituto Bacteriológico

São Mamede †

Rua Nova de S. Mamede

Rua Castilho

Rua do Salitre

AVENIDA Ⓜ

R. Manuel Jesus Coelho

Rua de S. José

Rua da Fé

Cç. M. Vento

Tv. Torel

Rua da Escola Politécnica

Parlamento

Jardim Botânico

3

2

Rua das Pretas

Av. da Liberdade

Rua Portas de Sto. Antão

Calçada de Santana

Cç. Enº Miguel Pais

R. do Monte Olivete

Tv. Salitre

a Alegria

Tv. de Santo António da Glória

Rosário

Rua da Alegria

Praça da Alegria

Rua das Taipas

Rua da Glória

Cç do Lavra

Elevador de Lavra

Praça Príncipe Real

R. D. Pedro V

R. Luisa Todi

R. S. Pedro Alcântara

Calçada da Glória

Elevador da Glória

start here

✉ (i)

RESTAURADORES Ⓜ

(i)

Palácio da Independência

Rua Vinha

Rua dos Mouros

Estação do Rossio

Teatro Nacional †

1 Praça dos Restauradores
2 Avenida da Liberdade
3 Restaurante Quebra-Mar
4 Praça Marquês de Pombal
5 Parque Eduardo VII
6 Jardim Amália Rodrigues
7 Restaurante Eleven

This is a refreshing walk to do on a Sunday morning, when the squares and avenue are relatively quiet and you can enjoy a leisurely stroll along the Avenida da Liberdade and through the Parque Eduardo VII, with its formal gardens and city views. START: Praça dos Restauradores.

Start your walk in the Praça dos Restauradores.

1 ★★ Praça dos Restauradores. Standing in this long square, you'll feel at the heart of the city as it's an easy stroll from here to the Avenida da Liberdade, Baixa, Alfama, and the Bairro Alto. Named after the restoration of power from the Spanish in 1640, the square has a monument at its center dedicated to those who fought. All across the square is a swathe of block paving with a knot-work design reminiscent of Portugal's maritime tradition. Whilst taking in the impressive architecture around you notice the **Eden Teatro**, a former theater built in the 1930s by Cassiano Branco. Today it's an apart-hotel (p 139), but retains the external Art Deco structure, friezes, and signs. The striking pink building next door, Palácio Foz, is a post-earthquake palace, today housing a tourist information center. *Metro: Restauradores. Bus: 2, 9, 36, 44, 45, 90, 91, 711, 732, 746. Elevador da Lavra. Elevador da Glória.*

2 ★★ Avenida da Liberdade. Built in 1879, this avenue brought Lisbon forward into the modern

Neptune statue on Avenida da Liberdade.

age, connecting the historic downtown with the new business district. Based on the style of the Champs Elysées in Paris, it's a pleasant strolling ground with a tree-lined sidewalk. Under the shade of the trees you'll pass various large hotels, cafes, banks, designer shops, restaurants, theaters, and early 20th-century town houses. Look out for no. 65, the birthplace of renowned Portuguese painter and sculptor Carlos Botelho (1899–1982). Further up, under a small forest of palms, a statue of Neptune sits on a bed of rocks with water pouring into a small pond below.

Praça Marques de Pombal.

3★★ **Restaurante Quebra-Mar.** This is one for seafood lovers, a restaurant renowned for the freshness of the produce. Expect traditional Portuguese fish dishes such as skewers of squid, grilled grouper, and barbecued sardines. Book ahead or come early to avoid disappointment. *Avenida da Liberdade, 77.* ☎ *21-346-4855. $$$.*

Whilst here, you may want to pop into the designer stores, which include Massimo Dutti on the right, and Mont Blanc, Hugo Boss, Ermenegildo Zegna, and Loewe on the left.

Look out for two cinemas: the Tivoli at no.188, a 1920s neoclassical delight where there are occasional kids' matinees and concerts; and the modernist Cinema São Jorge, opened in 1950 complete with orchestra, cinema organ, and air conditioning. The interior was remodeled and reopened in 2001. *Metro: Restauradores, Avenida, Pombal. Bus: 2, 9, 36, 44, 45, 90, 91, 711, 732, 746.*

4 ★ **Praça Marquês de Pombal.** More of a roundabout than a square, it's often so busy with traffic

that it's not easy to get to the center. Use the tunnels and pedestrian crossings to get to the park. *Metro: Marquês Pombal. Bus: 2, 9, 36, 44, 45, 90, 91, 711, 732, 746.*

5 ★★ **Parque Eduardo VII.** There's a tree-lined road on the bottom left side of the park, and if you come in July it'll be a swathe of purple flowers. The *Feira do Livro* (book fair) also takes place here then, with books for everyone in various languages. The downside is the stalls are housed in brightly colored temporary wooden huts that spoil the overall effect of the formal gardens. At any other time, you'll get a good view of the beds, bushes, and paths from the top or bottom of the park. An oasis of leisure and relaxation, it has sports facilities, greenhouses of tropical plants, ducks, geese and other wildfowl, plus a lakeside restaurant/cafe. On a clear day you can see all the way down the Avenida da Liberdade and even to the river.

Stop to see the Carlos Lopes Pavilion on the right-hand side of the park. Originally built in Brazil to mark the 100th anniversary of its independence in 1923, it was moved here and reconstructed in 1932. After years of hosting exhibitions and sports events, it has fallen into disrepair, disappointing considering the elaborate external *azulejos* panels depicting 18th-century style battle scenes. *Metro: Parque, Marquês Pombal. Bus: 1, 2, 11, 12, 18, 22, 23, 27, 31, 36, 42, 44, 45, 48, 51, 83, 90, 91, 113, 115, 718, 742, 746.*

⑥ ★★ Jardim Amália Rodrigues. This small garden has an intimate feel. Dedicated to *fadista* queen Amália Rodrigues (p 36), there's an eye-catching statue, *Maternidad*, by Colombian sculptor Fernando Botero at the entrance and across the other side of the pond a cafe with outdoor seating. *Alameda Cardeal Cerejeira, Alto do Parque. Open 24 hours a day. Metro: Parque. Bus: 203, 718, 742, 746.*

Elaborate azulejos on Carlos Lopes Pavilion in Parque Eduardo VII.

⑦ ★★★ Restaurante Eleven. This was the first restaurant in Lisbon to be awarded a Michelin star, and it tends to get booked up weeks ahead. Housed in a modern building, with panoramic city views, Eleven serves high-quality, contemporary Portuguese cuisine. *Rua Marquês de Fronteira, Jardim Amália Rodrigues. ☎ 21-386-2211. $$$$$ See also p 106.*

Purple blossom lines the edges of Parque Eduardo VII.

Baixa

0	200 yds
0	200 m

① Praça do Comércio
② Arco do Triunfo
③ Rua Augusta & the Baixa Streets
④ Elevador de Santa Justa
⑤ Praça da Figueira
⑥ Rossio Square
⑦ Ginjinha

The Baixa's grid-like layout makes it easy to navigate and a great place to get your bearings. With your back to the river, you'll see the Castelo de São Jorge and the Alfama to the right, the Chiado-Bairro Alto on the left, while straight ahead through Rossio Square leads to the Avenida da Liberdade. **START: Praça do Comércio. Metro: Baixa/Chiado. Tram: 12, 15. Bus: 2, 81, 92, 711, 713.**

① ★★ **Praça do Comércio.** In April 2010, the square reopened following a facelift that has given it easier access to the waterfront and improved it as a location for open-air exhibitions and concerts. Look out for the bronze (now green) statue of Dom José I with the medallion of the Baixa's 'architect', Pombal (see p 36) at the base. You can stroll in the shade of the arcaded edges of the square, pick up a Lisboa Card at the Lisbon Welcome Center and stop for coffee or lunch at the 200-year-old Café

Martinho da Arcada (see p 103). *Metro: Baixa-Chiado. Tram: 12, 15, 25. Bus: 2, 81, 92.*

② ★★ **Arco do Triunfo.** The Triumph Arch links Praça do Comércio and Rua Augusta, a project that took around 10 years to completion in 1873. It sports a collection of key Portuguese symbols from the royal coats of arms to famous historic figures including: Viriato, leader of the Lusitanians who fought against Roman occupation; Nuno Alvares Pereira, general during the fight for independence from Castille in the 14th century; explorer Vasco da Gama; and the Marquês de Pombal (see above). The Douro and Tagus rivers are also indicated, and the arch is topped with Glory, Genius, and Valor. *Praça do Comércio. Metro: Baixa-Chiado. Tram: 12, 15, 25. Bus: 2, 81, 92.*

❸ ★★ Rua Augusta & the Baixa Streets. This is the central, pedestrian-ized shopping thoroughfare of the Baixa. At the bottom end there are often stalls selling prints of Lisbon and artists offering to draw your caricature. The new Museum of Fashion and Design, MuDe, has also recently opened here (see p 40), giving the street an extra attraction and keeping it bang on trend. During good weather,

The Arco do Triunfo links the Praça de Comércio and Rua Augusta.

restaurants (mostly tourist-oriented ones) spill onto the street.

Follow Rua Augusta all the way to Praça Pedro V (Rossio), or zigzag through the side streets, brows-ing shops filled with Portu-guese shoes, handbags, and jewelry. Note the street names, given to match the trades of the people that worked here: *ouro* (gold), *douradores* (goldsmiths), *prata* (silver), *sapatelros* (cobblers), *correeiros* (saddlers), and *fanqueiros* (drapers). *Metro: Baixa-Chiado, Rossio. Tram: 12, 15, 25, 28. Bus: 2, 9, 36, 44, 45, 81, 90, 91, 92, 711.*

❹ ★★ Elevador de Santa Justa. I was struck by this bizarre iron tower the first time I saw it. Sandwiched into a Baixa side street, it was built by engineer Raoul

Gallery on Praça do Comércio.

The Baixa streets.

Mesnier du Ponsard in 1898–1901. Past rumors have claimed it was designed by Gustave Eiffel or that Ponsard was a student of his, but the former is pure hearsay and there's no proof of the latter. It's definitely worth taking a trip to the top of the lift for the view across the Baixa or to get to the Convento do Carmo, located by the upper level. *See p 9,* **6**.

Fountain on Rossio Square.

5 ★ **Praça da Figueira.** Located east of Rossio Square, this square is the 'scruffy' little brother. However, there are two renowned cafes here, Confeitaria Nacional on the south side and Pastelaria Suiça (see p 109) on the west (with another entrance on Rossio Square). There are also a few cheaper eateries, popular with the locals. The statue at the center of the square is Dom João I (1357–1433), but look out for the skateboarders as they can often fly across the center at a rate of knots. Head back along the south side of the square and look out for Manuel Tavares (see p 86), one of Lisbon's oldest and best-stocked wine shops. *Praça da Figueira. Metro: Baixa-Chiado, Restauradores. Tram: 12, 28. Bus: 2, 9, 36, 44, 45, 90, 91, 711.*

6 ★★ **Rossio Square.** This bustling space has popular cafes such as Nicola and Suiça (see p 104 and 109), bronze fountains, and stately neoclassical buildings.

The square wasn't always this pleasant; executions used to take place here, including the first *auto da fé* in which hundreds of people suspected of being 'non-Christian'

Dom João I Statue, Praça da Figueira.

were ruthlessly slaughtered. Fortunately, its function changed after the 1755 earthquake, and the inquisition building was eventually demolished to make way for the **Teatro Nacional de Dona Maria II** (see p 130). To the right of the theater there is now a small monument dedicated to the Jews that were slaughtered here.

Rossio is the square's old name, its official name today is Praça Dom Pedro IV. The **statue** on top of the pedestal was reputedly Emperor Maximilian of Mexico and rumor claims the monument was en route to Mexico when news arrived of his assassination, so the statue was quickly passed off as a Portuguese king instead.

At the northwest end of the square is **Rossio Station.** Built in 1886–7 by José Luís Monteiro, it's full of elaborate neo-Manueline features such as horseshoe-shaped doors lined with elaborate motifs, a carved figure of a knight at the center with a sword and shield, and the clock that tops the station. *Metro: Baixa-Chiado, Restauradores. Tram: 12, 28. Bus: 2, 9, 36, 44, 45, 90, 91, 711.*

7 ★★ Ginjinha. If you're like me, this hole-in-the-wall bar will easily become a regular aperitif stop-off during your stay. Get in line for your small, plastic cup of cherry brandy (ginjinha) and sip it with the collection of Lisboetas and visitors outside. *Largo São Domingos. See also p 116.$.*

Carvings on Rossio Station's façade.

Cais do Sodré—Chiado—Bairro Alto

0 200 yds
0 200 m

Jardim Botânico

Rua da Escola Politécnica
Parlamento
8 ★ finish here
Praça da Alegria
Av. da Liberdade
Rua da Glória
Rua das Taipas
Rua do Rosário
7

Rua Prazeres
Rua Nova Piedade
Praça Principe Real
R. D. Pedro V
6
R. Luisa Todi
Elevador da Glória

Calçada da Estrela
Rua de São Bento
Rua Ed. Coelho
BAIRRO ALTO
Tv. da Horta
Tv. de S. Pedro
R. de Alcântara
⊠ ⓘ
Ⓜ **RESTAURADORES**
ⓘ **Estação do Rossio** **Teatro Nacional**

Rua de Poiais de S. Bento
Rua do Vale
Tv. dos Inglesinhos
Rua do Século
R. da Atalaia
R. da Barroca
R. do Norte
R. da Misericórdia
ROSSIO
Pr. Dom Pedro IV
Ⓜ **ROSSIO**
Rua da Betesga

R. da Hera
R. do Loreto
R. da Trindade
Tv. do Carmo
R. do Carmo
R. de Sta. Justa
R. de Sta.

① Mercado da Ribeira
② Ascensor da Bica
③ Praça Luís de Camões
④ Teatro Nacional São Carlos
⑤ Convento do Carmo e Museu Arqueológico
⑥ Miradouro de São Pedro de Alcântara
⑦ Rua da Escola Politécnica
⑧ Jardim Botânico

③
R. da Horta Seca
CHIADO
Rua Garrett
Ⓜ **BAIXA-CHIADO**
BAIXA
Rua da Prata
Rua dos Correeiros

Calçada do Combro
R. da Bica
R. da Moeda
②
Rua do Alecrim
Rua António Maria Cardoso
Rua Nova do Almada
Rua Ivens
④

Praça D. Luís I
① start here
R. Nova Carv.
Rua Vitor Cordon
Praça do Município
Rua de S. Julião
Rua do Comércio
ⓘ

Ⓜ **CAIS DO SODRÉ**
Estação Cais do Sodré
Ⓟ
Rua do Arsenal
Praça do Comércio

ⓘ Information
⊠ Post Office
Ⓜ Metro Stop
Ⓟ Car Park

I like to think of this as an 'earthy' walk, taking in the sights and sounds of everyday Lisbon life in some of the most vibrant neighborhoods in the city. It starts in the fruit and vegetable market at Cais do Sodré and passes through the neighborhoods of Bairro Alto and Chiado, home to trendy shopping and a vibrant nightlife.
START: Cais do Sodré Market. Metro: Cais do Sodré. Tram: 15, 25.

① ★★ Mercado da Ribeira.
You have to get the timing right for the full impact of this lively market (also referred to as *Mercado 24 de Julho*). Come during the afternoon and all you'll find is empty stalls and the smell of fish as it's hosed away. It's even worth skipping breakfast to experience a slice of the action here. Come at 8am (or earlier) and you'll see stalls piled high with fresh fish and slippery squid, as well as meat, fruit, vegetables, and flowers.

You'll hear the cries of the stallholders as they sell their goods, see Portuguese women with their checkered aprons carrying their purchases, some of them on their heads. This is very much the real Lisbon. Upstairs there's a restaurant and bar, **Comida da Ribeira** and Ribeirarte, where you can have lunch and browse the regional crafts on sale at **A Loja de Artesano.** Turn left out of the back entrance, strolling right through the

Tiled wall in the lively Mercado da Ribeira.

pleasant square of Praça de São Paulo and left into Rua de São Paulo. Abruptly, away from the bustle of the market, you find yourself in a street where faded tile-clad houses display ornate iron balconies. ⏱ *30–45 min. Avenida 24 de Julho* ☎ *21-031-2600. Tues–Sat 5am–2pm. Tram: 5, 15, 18. Bus: 6, 35, 36, 40, 44, 45, 58, 82, 91.*

❷ ★ **Ascensor da Bica.** Keep your eyes peeled for the entrance to the elevator as it's easy to walk straight past. Buy your ticket from the man at the door and find yourself a seat onboard the small funicular train, or at least something to hold onto. It's a steep ride but great to be able to look out of the back window for a bird's-eye view of the neighborhood. The funicular slides up to the Bairro Alto, passing narrow residential streets and alleyways. It's good to get your feet back on firm ground as you really feel the pull downwards. ⏱ *5–10 min. Largo da Calhariz, Rua de São Paulo. Admission 1.30€ or free with Carris travel pass. Mon–Sat 7am–9pm; Sun & public holidays 9am–9pm.*

❸ ★ **Praça Luís de Camões.** Turn right from the elevator past several small cafes and shops until you reach a small square, where cars and trams criss-cross their way from the Bairro Alto to Estrela or down to the river. There are a few trendy fashion stores here, such as Diesel. Don't forget the statue at the center of the square, it represents Luís de Camões, the square's

Climb on board the funicular.

Praça Luis de Camões.

simple neoclassical combination of white brick archways and yellow painted walls above. Inside the auditorium is a rococo gem with a lavish royal box, but if you want to see it you'll have to buy a ticket to a performance (p 129). *Rua Serpa Pinto, 9.* ☎ *21-325-3045. www.saocarlos. pt. Tram: 28. Bus: 92.*

⑤ ★★★ **Convento do Carmo e Museu Arqueológico.** With an elevated position looking across the Baixa, you can see the Carmo Convent from many an angle, including the Castelo de São Jorge (see p 8). It is the roof, or lack of it, that is most apparent from afar, but inside you realize the walls are still standing. It could have been totally demolished or reconstructed, but it was kept, today housing a small archeological museum and a monument to the devastation caused by what is considered Europe's 'first modern disaster'. *See p 8,* ⑦.

namesake and one of Portugal's greatest writers (p 38). *Tram: 28. Bus: 92.*

④ ★★ **Teatro Nacional São Carlos.** Fronting onto a large and airy square with a cafe spilling out beside it, São Carlos Theater is a

⑥ ★ **Miradouro de São Pedro de Alcântara.** A perfect place to

Teatro Nacional São Carlos.

Miradouro de São Pedro de Alcântara.

finish your walk, this wide *miradouro* has a mini bedded park, maximizing its balcony view across the city. This is the place to take pictures—peer across to the hill opposite, where the Castelo de São Jorge crowns the Alfama for a spectacular view. *Rua Dom Pedro V. Metro: Restauradores. Elevador da Glória.*

❼ ★ Rua da Escola Politécnica. This street is a mixture of science, learning, arts, crafts, and shopping. Next to the **Botanic Gardens** (p 42) are the Science and Natural History museums, and opposite is the **Casa dos Tapetes de Arraiolos**, a carpet shop with a difference—you can buy a kit to make your own (see p 84). Further down the street you'll see a theater (Teatro Politecnica), antique shops, and second-hand book stores. *Rua da Escola Politécnica, 58. Metro: Rato. Bus: 58, 790.*

❽ ★★ Jardim Botânico. Great for escaping a hectic city day,

there's plenty to explore here. Don't miss the herb house by the entrance or the butterflies with hundreds of monarchs and pupae waiting to hatch. Cool off in the shade and catch a view through trees over the city. *See p 42,* **❻**.

Convento do Carmo.

Belém

Legend:
1. Jardim do Ultramar
2. Mosteiro dos Jerónimos
3. Centro Cultural de Belem
4. Torre de Belém
5. River Front
6. Padrão dos Descobrimentos
7. Cervejaria Portugália
8. Praça do Império

I never tire of visiting Belém with its sense of space and light and the attractive tree-lined squares and parks. Not even the railway line or busy Avenida de Brasília detract from the feel, and now there is a new walking and cycle route along the waterfront to add to the experience. START: **Tram stop: 15.**

1 ★★ Jardim do Ultramar.
Turn left out of the monastery and cross the square to the gateway at the right of the period property. This is a side entrance into the Ultramar Garden, also known as the Jardim-Museu Agrícola Tropical, home to some rare tropical trees and plants, and two avenues of palms that will lead you back and forth across the park. The park backs onto the **Palácio de Belém**, a former royal palace now home to the President of the Republic: you can't go in the palace but you can sneak a peek of its pink façade

through the trees. 🕐 *20–30 min. Calçada do Galvão.* ☎ *21-362-0210. May–Oct Tues–Fri 10am–5pm, Sat & Sun 11am–6pm, Nov–Apr Tues–Sun 10am–5pm. Train: Belém. Tram: 15. Bus: 27, 28, 29, 43, 49, 51, 112.*

2 ★★★ Mosteiro dos Jeróni-mos. Cross the road to the monastery, where you'll find good photo opportunities, particularly the church's south portal, the doorway of which is adorned with intricate Manueline details. If you go at lunchtime, it should be quiet enough to take in the carved tombs, columns, chapels, and vaulted ceiling in relative peace. Don't miss out on the exquisitely tranquil cloisters, also best in the afternoon, when the sunlight filters down into the courtyard. *See p 11,* ❸.

❸ ★★★ **Centro Cultural de Belém.** Walk along the length of the monastery, today housed by an archeological museum and maritime museum, before crossing over to the Centro Cultural de Belem. You'll see wine and gift shops along the side of the center (and more inside) and you can stop to see the Berardo Collection of Contemporary and Modern Art (p 46), enjoy lunch in the cafe (p 104) or book tickets for an evening performance. Otherwise wind your way through to the road on the far side. *See p 14,* ❼.

Sculpture on the exterior of the Mosteiro dos Jerónimos.

❹ ★★★ **kids Torre de Belém.** Walk along the Avenida da Brasilia and cross via the bridge to a small park. Away from the busy road, the mood becomes more tranquil as you stroll through a tree-shaded park. The Belém Tower is an island-like monument with castellated

Take in the Manueline details on the Torre de Belém.

Padrão dos Descobrimentos.

battlements. I like to sit on the curved steps where the water gently laps up.

The Torre de Belém was built under the orders of Dom Manuel I in 1515 as a fortress to guard the city, a role it held until 1580, when it became a prison under Spanish

Replica of Fairey III-B biplane Santa Cruz.

control. It continued to hold political prisoners after the Restoration in 1640 and later became a customs house. It was declared a UNESCO World Heritage Site (along with the Mosteiro dos Jerónimos) in 1983.

Take in the Manueline details of the tower from the external carved ropes and crosses to the animal heads and heraldic motifs. In the cellars the damp and dark bring to life the grim reality of being imprisoned here. *See also p 14,* **8**.

5 ★ **River Front.** Look out for the seaplane to the left of the tower, a replica of the Fairey III-B biplane *Santa Cruz* flown across the Atlantic in 1922. Nearby a new riverside path begins, which has transformed the waterfront walk. Now you can wind your way around the marina, past the luxury **Altis Belem Hotel** (p 138). (The path continues all the way to Cais do Sodré.)

You'll see waterfront restaurants such as Cervejaria Portugalia (p 105) and Ja Sei, where you can have a

Praça do Império.

direct view of the Padrão dos Descobrimentos.

6 ★★★ Padrão dos Descobrimentos. Carefully crafted characters line this monument, made in the shape of a *caravela* boat—a popular explorers' vessel during the 15th and 16th centuries. Look out for depictions of explorers as well as royalty, mathematicians, writers, and artists. Benches on either side of the monument let you sit and take in the view of the river. Beyond you can hear the 'clink-clink' of yachts moored at the marina. *See p 15,* **9**.

7 ★ Cervejaria Portugália. Part of a chain, this restaurant offers decent Portuguese cuisine at reasonable prices. This restaurant has a prime waterfront position with a terrace facing the Padrão. You can't miss the bright white exterior perched on the water. *Avenida Brasilia, Edificio Espelho de Agua.* 📞 *21-303-2700. $$–$$$. See also p 105.*

8 ★ Praça do Império. From the Padrão, head towards the road and go through the tunnel to cross the road to the square. On hot days there's often a mobile ice-cream seller here. Stroll through the square, draped with cypress and olive trees, with Portuguese-style black-and-white stone pathways that lead past grand, central fountains. To your left you'll see the angular modernity of Centro Cultural de Belém (p 14), contrasting with the elaborate detail of the 15th-century Mosteiro dos Jerónimos (p 11) ahead

Portugalia Restaurant on the river front.

Rato—Amoreiras—Estrela

① Largo do Rato
② Parque das Amoreiras
③ Amoreiras Shopping Center
④ Campo de Ourique
⑤ Basilica da Estrela
⑥ Assembleia da República
⑦ Rua de São Bento

This is a diverse walk, with a little sightseeing and as much shopping as you wish. It passes through an eclectic neighborhood from the busy junction of Largo do Rato, uphill to the aqueduct and Amoreiras shopping center, through the Campo de Ourique neighborhood and downhill past the Basilica da Estrela before a climb uphill along the antique-filled Rua de São Bento. START: **Metro: Rato. Bus: 6, 9, 58, 74.**

① ★ **Largo do Rato.** This square is a departure point, not just for the metro station underneath (check out the abstract *azulejos* panels by Arpad Szènés and Vieira da Silva) and the bus station at its center, but also because of the various roads that lead off it. Around the edge are inexpensive eateries, popular with locals and rarely frequented by tourists. Walk to the top of Rua Alexandre Herculano and you can delve into the Charcutaria Brasil for an even cheaper packed lunch of fresh

cheese, ham, and bread. *Largo do Rato. Metro: Rato. Bus: 6, 9, 58, 74.*

② ★★ **Parque das Amoreiras.** Walk uphill along Rua das Amoreiras to find this park, named after the mulberry trees once planted here to feed the silk worms at the local factory, now long gone. Look up to see a small section of the city's aqueduct towering above; down below are 18th-century *azulejos* panels by António Oliveira Bandeiras. *Praça*

Explore the shops around Rato.

das Amoreiras. Open 24 hours a day. Metro: Rato. Bus: 58, 74.

☕ Amoreiras Shopping Center. Continue uphill and turn left for this large modern shopping center (p 83) offering a large selection of cafes, sandwich bars, and restaurants. There's something for all budgets and tastes from soup and salad to Mexican. *Avenida Engenheiro Duarte Pacheco.* ☎ *21-381-0200.* *$–$$$$.*

④ Campo de Ourique. Turn right out of the exit beside Benetton and follow the road to the right, turning left at Rua Ferreira Borges. This is the start of the residential Campo de Ourique area, which has a lively old-town feel and a strong local community. Shops and cafes line the main streets and you can zigzag your way around the galleries and twice-weekly food market (open Mon and Sat) on Rua Coelho da Rocha.

⑤ Basilica da Estrela. Walk down Rua Domingos Sequeira to the basilica, perhaps stopping to watch the ducks in the gardens opposite.

The basilica's dome and towers are a city landmark and can be seen from the castle. It was built on the orders of Queen Mary I in the 18th century, as thanks to God for giving her a son, Jose, who unfortunately died before the basilica was completed. Once your eyes have adjusted to the dark, look out for the queen's tomb inside. *Largo da Estrela.* ☎ *21-396-0915. Free admission. Daily 8am–8pm.*

See the 18th-century azulejos panels around the aqueduct in Parque das Amoreiras.

The towers of the Basilica da Estrela.

6 Assambleia da República. Before you get to the bottom of the hill, take a peek over the wall to see the formal gardens at the back of the parliament building. Continue to the front of the large, white neoclassical building, also known as the Palace of Sao Bento, originally earmarked to house a Benedictine monastery. Construction coincided with the 1755 earthquake and it was severely damaged. It has been home to the Portuguese Parliament since 1820. The front of the building is striking for its tall, white neoclassical columns, and statues representing strength, justice, prudence, and temperance. It is not generally open for visits but hosts occasional exhibitions. *Palácio de São Bento.* ☎ 21-391-9000.

Fish at a market in the Campo de Ourique area.

7 Rua de São Bento. This street runs to the right of the parliament building. Expect a steep climb uphill to finish the walk, but you can go slowly, browsing the many antique and art shops along the way. You'll pass the **Casa-Museu Amalia Rodrigues**, once home to Portugal's most renowned fado singer, www.amalia.com. ●

Shopping Best Bets

Best **Bric-à-Brac Market**
★★★ Feira da Ladra, *Campo de Santa Clara (p 82)*

Best **Wine Shop**
★★★ Manuel Tavares, *Rua da Batesga, 1A-B (p 87)*

Best **Leather Goods**
★★★ Loewe, *Avenida da Liberdade, 185 (p 88)*

Best **Azulejos (tiles)**
★★★ Fabrica Sant'Anna, *Rua do Alecrim, 96 (p 83)*

Best **Lisbon Souvenirs**
★★ Artesanato do Tejo, *Rua do Arsenal, 25 (p 86)*

Best **Antiques**
★★★ Murteira Antiguidades, *Rua Augusta Rosa (p 82)*

Best **Street Shopping**
★★ Baixa, *Rua Augusta (p 84)*

Best **Designer Shopping**
★★ Avenida da Liberdade and Rua do Carmo *(p 84)*

Best **Art Gallery**
★ Galeria Pedro Serrenho, *Rua Almeida e Sousa, 21A (p 82)*

Best **Department Store**
El Corte Inglés, *Between Avenidas Antonio Augusto e Aguiar and Marquês da Fronteira e Sidónio Pais (p 83)*

Best **Mall for Kids**
★★ Vasco da Gama, *Parque das Nações (p 84)*

Best **Jewelry**
★★ Augusto Joalheiros, *Rua Augusta, 106–8 (p 87)*

Best **Portuguese Designer Store**
★★★ Ana Salazar, *Rua do Carmo, 87 (p 85)*

Best **Music Shop**
★★ Louie Louie, *Rua Nova da Trindade (p 88)*

Best **Hat Shop**
★★ Azevedo Rua, *Dom Pedro IV, 72–73 (p 85)*

Postcard Shop in the Alfama.

City Center Shopping

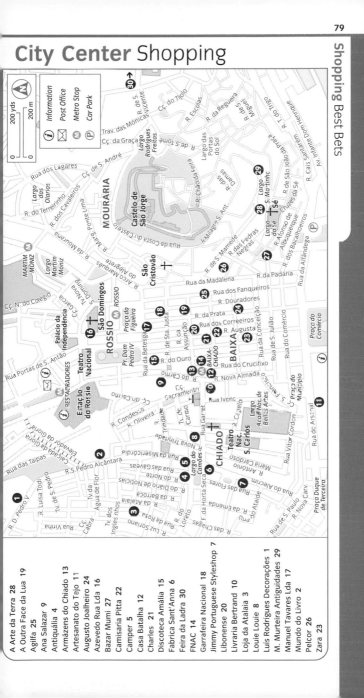

A Arte da Terra 28
A Outra Face da Lua 19
Aglifa 25
Ana Salazar 9
Antiquália 4
Armazéns do Chiado 13
Artesanato do Tejo 11
Augusto Joalheiro 24
Azevedo Rua Lda 16
Bazar Mumi 27
Camisaria Pitta 22
Camper 5
Casa Batalha 12
Charles 21
Discoteca Amália 15
Fabrica Sant'Anna 6
Feira da Ladra 30
FNAC 14
Garrafeira Nacional 18
Jimmy Portuguese Styleshop 7
Libonense 20
Livraria Bertrand 10
Loja da Atalaia 3
Louie Louie 8
Luis Rodrigues Decorações 1
M. Murteira Antiguidades 29
Manuel Tavares Lda 17
Mundo do Livro 2
Pelcor 26
Zara 23

North of Center Shopping

Amoreiras Shopping **2**
Casa dos Tapetes de Arraiolos **4**
Centro Colombo **10**
Charcutaria Brasil **3**
El Corte Inglés **8**
Galeria Pedro Serrenho **1**
Leninha **9**
Linho Bordado **7**
Loewe **5**
Vasco da Gama Shopping **6**

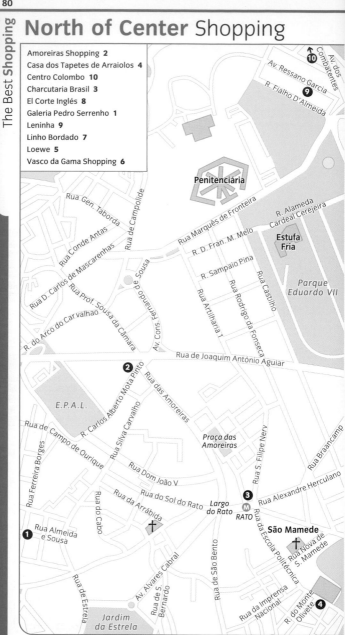

R. Dr. Nicolau de Bettencourt
Rua Marquês Sá da Landeira
Av. Cod.e de Valbom
Av. Miguel Bobarda
Av. João Crisóstomo
Av. da República
Av. D. Filipa de Vilhena

0   200 yds
0   200 m

M Metro Stop

Instituto Superior Technico

SÃO SEBASTIÃO M

❽

Av. António Augusto Aguiar
Av. Sidónio Pais
Av. do Duque d'Ávila
Rua Pinheiro Chagas
Av. Luís Bívar
R. Sebastião da Pedreira
Rua Filipe Folque
Rua Latino Coelho
Rua 5 de Outubro

SALDANHA M

SALDANHA
Praça Duque de Saldanha

Av. Defensores de Chaves

Rua Açores

Rua Ponta Delgada
Rua Cidade da Horta
Rua Pascoal de Melo

❼

PARQUE

PICOAS M
Rua Andrade Curvo
Rua Tomás Ribeiro
R. Eng. V. da Silva
K. A. Taborda
Av. Casal Ribeiro
R. Alm. Barroso

Praça José Fontana

R. Esc. Med. Veterinária

To Parque das Nações (see inset) →

Av. Fontes Pereira de Melo
Rua de Santa Marta
Rua Camilo Castelo Branco
Av. Duque de Loulé
Rúa Cônde Redondo
Rua Bernardim Ribeiro
R. Joaq. Bonifácio
Rua Gomes Freire
Rua de Dona Estefânia
R. Jacinta Marto

Praça Marquês do Pombal

MARQUÊS DE POMBAL M

Rua Duque de Palmela
Rua Mouzinho da Silveira
Rua Castilho
Av. da Liberdade
Rua Rodrigues Sampaio
Rua de Santa Marta
Rua de S. José

ESTEFÂNIA

Rua Barata Salgueiro
❺

Rua do Salitre

AVENIDA M

Jardim Botânico

Tv. do Salitre
Tv. do Rosário
Av. da Liberdade

Praça da Alegria

Parque das Nações

M ORIENTE
❻
Av. do Índico
Av. do Pacífico
Alameda dos Oceanos
R. do Caribe
Av. Dom João II
R. da Centieira
Báltico
R. do Mar do Norte
Pólo Sul
Av. do
R. do

Pavilhão Atlântico

Rossio dos Olivias

Doca dos Olivais

Oceanário

0   300 yds
0   300 m

Lisbon **Shopping A to Z**

Antiques & Art

★ **Antiquália** BAIRRO ALTO This store stocks some choice pieces of furniture, much of it from the Far East, as well as a good variety of lighting, porcelain, and ceramics. *Praça Luís de Camões, 37.* ☎ *21-342-3260. AE, DC, MC, V. Tram: 28. Map p 79.*

★ **Feira da Ladra** ALFAMA Come here early on a Tuesday or Saturday morning to rummage among the stalls. As they say, one man's rubbish is another's gold, so you might find that elusive old accordion you were looking for. *Campo de Santa Clara. Tram: 12, 28. Map p 79.*

★ **Galeria Pedro Serrenho** CAMPO DE OURIQUE A bright and modern gallery with a collection of contemporary fine art works by Portuguese and international artists, many of them abstract but all very different in style. *Rua Almeida e Sousa, 21A.* ☎ *21-393-0714. www. galeriapedroserrenho.com. AE, MC, V. Metro: Rato. Map p 80.*

Have a good rummage at the Feira da Ladra.

★★ **M. Murteira Antiguidades** ALFAMA Pieces range from 15th-century sculptures and 17th-century furniture to 20th-century fine art. These are investment pieces so this shop is for serious collectors rather than casual browsers. *Rua Augusta Rosa, 19–21.* ☎ *21-886-3851. www. murteira-antiguidades.com. AE, DC, MC, V. Tram: 12, 28. Map p 79.*

Books

★★ **FNAC** BAIXA/CHIADO FNAC is a large and reliable store for books, including some in English, as well as music, electronics, and concert tickets. You can even pick up a book and browse through it in the cafe. As well as the Baixa, you'll find stores in most of the large shopping centers. *Armázens do Chiado, Rua do Carmo, 2.* ☎ *707-313-435. www. fnac.pt. AE, MC, V. Metro: Baixa-Chiado. Map p 79.*

★ **Livraria Bertrand** BELEM Bertrand is a chain with stores in just about every shopping center, plus Bairro Alto and the Belém Cultural Center. There's a wide selection of subjects, with some titles in English. *Rua Garrett, 17.* ☎ *21-347-6122. AE, DC, MC, V. Metro: Baixa-Chiado. Map p 79. CCB, Praça do Imperio.* ☎ *21-364-5637. AE, DC, MC, V. Tram: 15.*

★★ **Mundo do Livro** BAIRRO ALTO A veritable treasure trove of out-of-print books in various languages, along with ancient maps and authentic and reproduction prints. They'll also mount and frame them according to your specifications. *Largo da Trindade, 12.* ☎ *21-346-9951. www.mlivro.com. AE, MC, V. Metro: Rossio. Map p 79.*

Ceramics, Pottery & Tiles

★★ Bazar Mumi ALFAMA This store next to the cathedral sells genuine hand-painted tiles. You can usually see the artists at work and request commissioned pieces. *Largo de Santo António da Sé.* ☎ *21-887-0089. AE, DC, MC, V. Tram: 28. Map p 79.*

★★★ Fabrica Sant'Anna BAIRRO ALTO Simply the best place to buy tiles to take home. They're all handmade and absolutely exquisite, from the functional style to elaborate panels covered in still life or pastoral scenes; also ceramic pots, vases, and basins. You can visit the factory or even take a class yourself, but do phone first. *Rua do Alecrim, 96.* ☎ *21-342-2537. www.fabrica-santanna.com. MC, V. Metro: Baixa-Chiado. Map p 79.*

Factory and 2nd showroom: Calçada da Boa-Hora, 96. ☎ *21-363-292. MC, V. Tram: 15.*

Department Stores/Shopping Centers

★★ Amoreiras Shopping AMOREIRAS Between the business district and Campo de Ourique, this

The eye-catching Amorieras Shopping Centre.

Armázens do Chiado.

shopping center is housed in an eye-catching modern mirrored building. The mall has 275 shops, including Habitat, Macmoda, and Pão de Açucar supermarket, plus a multiplex cinema and international clothing chains such as Zara. *Avenida Engenheiro Duarte Pacheco.* ☎ *21-381-0200. www.amoreiras.com. Metro: Rato, Pombal. Map p 80.*

★★ Armázens do Chiado CHIADO This compact shopping center has 41 stores from FNAC to Adolfo Dominguez, plus several restaurants. In the heart of the city, you can enter via the ground floor in the Baixa and exit in the Chiado. *Rua do Carmo.* ☎ *21-321-0600. www.armazensdochiado.com. Metro: Baixa-Chiado. Map p 79.*

★★★ Centro Colombo LUZ The largest shopping center in the Iberian peninsula, it boasts more than 420 shops, a supermarket, 60 restaurants, a multiplex cinema with 10 screens, amusements, and a health club. *Avenida Lusiada.* ☎ *21-711-3600. www.colombo.pt. Metro: Colegio Militar. Map p 80.*

★★ El Corte Inglés PARQUE Spain's largest department store found its way to Lisbon a few years

Best Shopping Areas

Lisbon's Baixa district is a traditional shopping area with international chains and home-grown leather and jewelry stores. On Rua de Ouro, some stores link to the **Chiado** and its compact mall, Armazens do Chiado. Along Rua do Carmo and Rua Garrett are international and local designer stores, but for high-end designer fashion, browse the **Avenida da Liberdade.** In **Saldanha,** you'll find the quality Spanish department store El Corte Inglés, along with other small renowned stores all the way up to **Campo Grande.** For antiques, rugs, and second-hand books, start at **Rato** and stroll along Rua de São Bento or Rua da Escola Politécnica towards the Bairro Alto. Rummage for bargains at the Feira da Ladra market in the **Alfama** on Tuesdays and Saturdays. For large shopping malls, make a bee-line for **Amoreiras Shopping,** near Rato, take the metro to **Oriente** for Vasco da Gama Shopping or **Colégio Militar** for Colombo Shopping.

ago. Everything from fashion and furnishings to a supermarket and restaurant means you could spend the whole day here if you wished. *Between Avenidas Antonio Augusto e Aguiar and Marquês da Fronteira e Sidónio Pais.* ☎ *21-371-1700. www.elcorteingles.pt. Metro: São Sebastião. Map p 80.*

The Vasco da Gama shopping experience.

★★ Vasco da Gama Shopping
PARQUE DAS NACOES   Lisbon's newest mall at the time of writing, an attractive, large glass building by Oriente train station and leading out into the Parque das Nações. It has around 120 stores, a supermarket, 36 restaurants, a 10-screen cinema, health club, and a kids' play area. *Avenida Dom João II.* ☎ *1-893-0600. www.centrovascodagama.pt. Metro: Oriente. Map p 80.*

Designer Home Goods & Furnishings
★★ Agilfa BAIXA   There's everything from fine crystal glassware and porcelain to cooking utensils and cutlery at this Portuguese store. *Rua dos Fanqueiros, 226–232.* ☎ *91-739-1532. www.algifa.pt. AE, DC, MC, V. Metro: Baixa-Chiado. Map p 79.*

★★★ Casa dos Tapetes de Arraiolos BAIRRO ALTO   For the past couple of decades this company has been making rugs and tapestries, some with an antique style. You can buy them ready made from

Check out A Outra Face da Lua for quality vintage clothes and paraphernalia.

this store or in kit form to make your own. *Rua da Imprensa Nacional, 116F.* ☎ *21-396-3354. www,casa tapetesarraiolos.com. AE, DC, MC, V. Tram: 28. Map p 80.*

★ **Loja da Atalaia** BAIRRO ALTO This store is renowned for its immaculate and stylish retro furniture, mostly from the 1950s to the 1980s. *Rua da Atalaia, 71.* ☎ *21-882-2578. www.lojadatalaia.com. AE, DC, MC, V. Tram: 28. Map p 79.*

★ **Luís Rodrigues Decorações** BAIRRO ALTO If you admire Portuguese elegance, you can find everything you need here to furnish your abode from carpets to furniture. *Rua Dom Pedro V, 84.* ☎ *21-346-8836. www.lordeco.com. AE, DC, MC, V. Metro: Rossio, Restauradores. Map p 79.*

Fashion & Accessories
★★★ **Ana Salazar** CHIADO Ana Salazar has been making waves in the Portuguese fashion industry since the 1970s. Her designs are still at the forefront of cutting-edge fashion. Be prepared to splash out if you want something from her latest collection. *Rua do Carmo, 87.* ☎ *21-347-2289. www.anasalazar.pt. AE,*

MC, V. Metro: Baixa-Chiado. Map p 79.

★★★ **A Outra Face da Lua** BAIXA/ALFAMA An Aladdin's cave of vintage finds from 1920s' flapper dresses to seventies disco chic. Designer Carla Belchior also sells her recycled clothing here—alongside an interesting collection of tin toys and wallpaper. *Rua da Assunção, 22.* ☎ *21-886-3430. www. aoutrafacedalua.com. MC, V. Metro: Baixa-Chiado. Map p 79. Alfama store: Calçada do Correio Velho, 7.* ☎ *21-886-3186. AE, DC, MC, V. Tram: 28.*

★ **Azevedo Rua Lda** BAIXA This traditional shop on Rossio Square is the kind of store frequented by elegant older gentlemen although the younger generation shouldn't bypass it completely—there's plenty of wearable caps and berets for the fashion conscious. *Praça Dom Pedro IV, 72–73.* ☎ *21-347-0817. AE, MC, V. Metro: Rossio. Map p 79.*

★★ **Camisaria Pitta** BAIXA This is one of Lisbon's oldest men's shirt shops, with attentive shop assistants who will help you find whatever style you need. They also do

Traditional hat shop on Azevedo Rua.

alterations and tailor-made suits. *Rua Augusta, 195.* ☎ *21-342-7526. AE, DC, MC, V. Metro: Baixa-Chiado. Map p 79.*

★ **Pelcor** BAIXA   Everything in this shop is made from Portuguese cork, making it more unusual than most of the touristic gift shops. Choose from brief cases and hand-bags to cushion covers, hats, and belts. *Rua das Pedras Negras. 32* ☎ *21-304-9727. AE, MC, V. Tram: 28. Map p 79.*

★ **Zara** BAIXA PARQUE   These days no city (or lady's wardrobe) would be complete without Zara. Reasonably priced, it has all your basic tops, suits, eveningwear, shoes, and accessories. Branches located in all the main shopping areas and malls. *Rua Augusta, 71–81.* ☎ *21-324-1400. AE, DC, MC, V. Metro: Baixa-Chiado. Map p 79. Other location: Avenida António Aguiar, 134.* ☎ *21-312-9690. Metro: Parque, São Sebastião.*

Gifts
★★ **A Arte da Terra** ALFAMA   Located in a historic building with vaulted ceilings, right in the heart of the Alfama, this store prides itself on selling some of the best samples of regional crafts from decorated tiles to paintings of Lisbon. *Rua de Augusto Rosa.* ☎ *21-274-5975. www.aartedaterra.pt. AE, MC, V. Tram: 28. Map p 79.*

★ **Artesanato do Tejo** BAIXA   Part of the Lisbon Welcome Center, this handicraft shop is located round the corner in Rua do Arsenal. It sells Lisbon-themed T-shirts, tiles, jewelry made by local artists, *fado* CDs, and tourist guides. *Rua do Arsenal, 25.* ☎ *21-031-2820. AE, DC, MC, V. Metro: Baixa-Chiado. Map p 79.*

★ **Jimmy Portuguese Style-shop** BAIRRO ALTO   If you want to steer away from the usual 'tourist-oriented' gifts, then this might be the place for you. It's all made in Portugal but everything has a much more designer and pop feel, with quirky handbags, bright cockerels in a range of colors, and trendy chan-delier lights. *Rua das Flores.* ☎ *91-898-4695. AE, DC, MC, V. Metro: Baixa-Chiado. Map p 79.*

★★ **Linho Bordado** SALDANHA   A little off the main tourist route, but worth a visit for its traditional hand-made lace and embroidery. There is usually something to suit most bud-gets from bread basket liners to sheets. *Ria Cidade da Horta, 36A.* ☎ *21-314-0279. AE, MC, V. Metro: Saldanha, Arroios. Map p 80.*

Gourmet Food & Drink
★ **Charcutaria Brasil** RATO   A little off the tourist trail, this store is tellingly used widely by the locals. You'll find picnic worthy treats from tasty *presunto* (cured meat), goat's cheese, freshly cooked chicken from the spit, and fresh fruit to bottles of water and wine. *Rua Alexandre Her-culano, 90.* ☎ *21-388-5644. AE, DC, MC, V. Metro: Rato. Map p 80.*

with a traditional wood-framed shop front, it has select Portuguese wines and international liquors, as well as *chouriços*, meats and cheeses from the delicatessen, colorful displays of glacé fruits and mouthwatering chocolates. *Rua da Batesga, 1A-B.* ☎ *21-342-4209. www.manuel tavares.com. AE, DC, MC, V. Metro: Rossio. Map p 79.*

Jewelry

★★ Augusto Joalheiro BAIXA This traditional jewelry shop is on the Baixa's busiest street. Alongside silver and gold jewelry, it sells quality watches and silverware. *Rua Augusta, 106–8.* ☎ *21-346-0616. AE, DC, MC, V. Metro: Baixa-Chiado. Map p 79.*

Casa Batalha CHIADO This family-run store has been in business since the 17th century. Expect quality goods and a personal service. They also have a store in Amoreiras shopping center. *Armazens do Chiado.* ☎ *21-342-7313. AE, DC, MC, V. Metro: Baixa-Chiado. Other branch: Shopping Amoreiras.* ☎ *21-691-8912. Map p 79.*

A shop's display of port and wine.

★★ Garrafeira Nacional BAIXA A good range of national and international wines as well as port and Madeira, and spirits such as *aguadente* (fire water). *Rua de Santa Justa, 18.* ☎ *21-887-9080. www.garrafeiranacional.com. MC, V. Metro: Baixa-Chiado. Map p 79.*

★★ Manuel Tavares Lda BAIXA One of the city's oldest stores, and

The Shopping Fine Print

Portugal isn't as strict over its traditional shopping hours as its neighbor, Spain, but some stores do still close for a couple of hours at lunchtime, usually from 1pm–3pm. The upside is most shops stay open until 8pm or 9pm. In the shopping centers, you can shop any day from 10am till midnight. Markets tend to open around breakfast time or earlier and close around lunchtime.

The tourist office offers a Shopping Card, which you can purchase from any of their outlets for 3.70€ for 24 hours or 5.80€ for 72 hours. It offers discounts of between 5% and 15% at around 200 stores in the Baixa, Chiado, and Avenida da Liberdade. See www.askmelisboa.com for more information.

For information on sales tax and related rebates for non EU residents, see p 169.

Fado Recordings.

Music
★★★ Discoteca Amália BAIXA
If you want to take some *fado* music home with you, then there's no better place than this store. Named after the diva of all *fadistas*, Amália Rodrígues, it has both traditional and modern recordings. You can always ask at the counter for advice. *Rua Aurea, 274.* ☎ *21-342-1485. MC, V. Metro: Baixa-Chiado. Map p 79.*

FNAC See books.

★★ Louie Louie CHIADO
One of three shops in Portugal, this branch sells new and used vinyl and CDs. Rummage among a wide range of genres from jazz to pop, rock to *fado*. You can also buy concert tickets here. *Rua Nova da Trindade. www.louie louie.biz.* ☎ *21-347-2232. MC, V. Metro: Baixa-Chiado. Map p 79.*

Shoes & Leather Goods
★★ Camper BAIRRO ALTO
Camper shoes have become renowned in the past decade for their distinctive curved soles, cool round toes, and range of colors. *Praça Luis de Camões.* ☎ *21-342-1178. AE, DC, MC, V. Tram: 28. Map p 79.*

★★ Charles BAIXA
A Portuguese chain of leather stores (there are eight in Lisbon alone), stocking quality leather clothing for men and women, as well as a wide selection of accessories such as bags and shoes. These stores also have a more affordable range for smaller budgets. *Rua Augusta 275-A.* ☎ *21-342-0700. AE, MC, V. Metro: Baixa Chiado.*
Rua Augusta 109. ☎ *21-347-7360. AE, MC, V. Metro: Baixa Chiado.*
Rua do Carmo, 105. ☎ *21-342-5500. AE, MC, V. Metro: Baixa Chiado. Map p 79.*

★★★ Leninha SALDANHA
Just a short walk from the Gulbenkian Museum, this is more than a shoe shop. As well as various brands of footwear for both men and women it stocks a few handbags, briefcases, and gloves. *Avenida Ressano Garcia, 11-D.* ☎ *21-387-7947. AE, DC, MC, V. Metro: Saldanha, Praça de Espanha. Map p 80.*

★★ Libonense BAIXA
This is an old-fashioned shoe shop, the kind where you get personal attention and quality leather footwear. Expect classic styles for men, women, and children. *Rua Augusta 202–204.* ☎ *21-342-6712. AE, MC, V. Metro: Baixa Chiado. Map p 79.*

★★★ Loewe AVENIDA
A Spanish store that sells luxury leather goods and fashion. Located on the ground floor of the Tivoli Hotel—expect to pay for the quality. *Avenida da Liberdade, 185.* ☎ *21-354-0050. AE, DC, MC, V. Metro: Avenida. Map p 80.* ●

Parque **Eduardo VII**

| 0 | 200 yds |
| 0 | 200 m |

Ⓜ Metro Stop

SÃO SEBASTIÃO Ⓜ

Penitenciária

Rua Pinheiro Chagas
Av. Luís Bivar
Rua Filipe Folque
Rua Tomás Ribeiro
Av. António Augusto Aguiar
Av. Sidónio Pais
R. Sebastião da pedreira

Rua de Campolide
Rua Marquês de Fronteira
R. Alameda Cardeal Cerejeira
R. D. Fran. M. Melo
Ⓜ PARQUE

R. Sampaio Pina
Rua Castilho

Rua Rodrigo da Fonseca
Rua Artilharia 1
Parque Eduardo VII

Av. Cons. Fernando de Sousa
Av. Fontes Pereira de Melo

Rua de Joaquim António Aguiar
Praça Marquês de Pombal

Av. Duque de Loulé
Rua Camilo Castelo Branco

MARQUÊS DE POMBAL Ⓜ
Av. da Liberdade

① Estufas
② Formal Gardens
③ Jardim Amália Rodrigues
④ Clube VII

From the foot of the **Avenida da Liberdade** you can see the formal layout of **Parque Eduardo VII,** the city center's foremost stretch of greenery, crisscrossed by paths and carefully trimmed hedges. On Sundays it seems that half the city is here strolling, playing sport, taking their kids to the play areas, picnicking, or feeding ducks on the lake. START: **Metro: Parque, Pombal. Bus: 1, 2, 11, 12, 18, 22, 23, 27, 31, 36, 42, 44, 45, 48, 51, 83, 90, 91, 113, 115, 718, 742, 746.**

The lake and greenhouses.

The formal gardens of Parque Eduardo VII.

① ★ **Estufas.** The park's *estufas* (greenhouses) of tropical plants are well worth the small entrance fee. The unheated Estufa Fria contains flora from around the world, the paths lead you by waterfalls, ponds and grottos. In the heated Estufa Quente (hothouse), you'll find coffee and mango plants, and the tiny Estufa Doce houses cacti such as *golden barrel* and *aloe vera*. ☎ 21-388-2278. *Admission 1.65€, .83€ youth card holders, seniors; free under 12s, Lisbon Card holders. Open Apr–Sept 9am–5:30pm; Oct–Mar 9am–4:30pm.*

② **Formal Gardens.** The park's most eye-catching features (and the main area of the park) are the beds, hedges, and pathways of the formal gardens, visible from far away. Stroll along the pathways and stop for ice cream, coffee, or lunch at the lakeside.

③ ★ **Jardim Amália Rodrigues.** This small garden is dedicated to Amália Rodrigues, Lisbon's much-feted fado *queen* (p 36). There's a café-bar looking across a lake, a bronze of a mother and child by Colombian sculptor Carlos Botero called *Maternidade,* and the Michelin-starred restaurant, Eleven (p 106). *Alameda Cardeal Cerejeira, Alto do Parque. Open 24 hours a day. Bus: 203, 718, 742, 746.*

④ **Clube VII.** If you want a workout in the gym, a swim in the indoor pool, or a game of tennis, this is a particularly well set-up sports facility in the city center. Guests of Le Meridien Park Atlantic Lisbon, can take advantage of the hotel's membership here. *Parque Eduardo VII.* ☎ 808-277-288; *www.club evii.com. Open Tues–Fri 7am–10:30pm; Sat 9am–9pm; Sun & public holidays 10am–6pm.*

Maternidade sculpture by Carlos Botero.

City Center Gardens

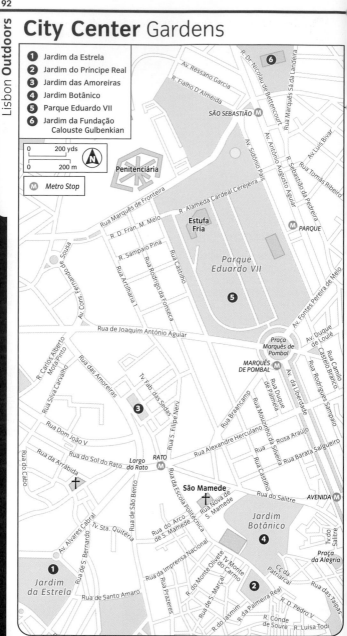

1. Jardim da Estrela
2. Jardim do Príncipe Real
3. Jardim das Amoreiras
4. Jardim Botânico
5. Parque Eduardo VII
6. Jardim da Fundação Calouste Gulbenkian

| 0 | 200 yds |
| 0 | 200 m |

Metro Stop

Penitenciária

SÃO SEBASTIÃO 🇲

Av. Ressano Garcia

R. Fialho D'Almeida

R. Dr Nicolau de Bettencourt

Rua Marquês Sá da Bandeira

Av. Luís Bívar

Rua Tomás Ribeiro

Rua Sebastião da Pedreira

Av. António Augusto Aguiar

Av. Sidónio Pais

R. Alameda Cardeal Cerejeira

Rua Marquês de Fronteira

R. D. Fran. M. Melo

R. Sampaio Pina

Rua Artilharia 1

Rua Rodrigo da Fonseca

Rua Castilho

Av. Fernando de Sousa

Av. Cons.

Estufa Fria

Parque Eduardo VII

5

🇲 PARQUE

Rua de Joaquim António Aguiar

Praça Marquês de Pombal

MARQUÊS DE POMBAL 🇲

Av. Fontes Pereira de Melo

Av. Duque de Loulé

Rua Camilo Castelo Branco

Rua Rodrigues Sampaio

R. Carlos Alberto Mota Pinto

Rua Silva Carvalho

Rua das Amoreiras

Rua Dom João V

Rua do Sol do Rato

Rua da Arrábida

Rua do Cabo

Tv. Fab. das Sedas

Rua S. Filipe Nery

3

Rua Braancamp

Rua Duque de Palmela

Rua Mouzinho da Silveira

Av. da Liberdade

Rua Alexandre Herculano

Rua da Rosa Araújo

Rua Barata Salgueiro

Largo do Rato

RATO 🇲

São Mamede

Rua da Escola Politécnica

Rua de São Bento

Rua Nova de S. Mamede

Rua Castilho

Rua do Salitre

AVENIDA 🇲

Av. Álvares Cabral

Tv. Sta. Quitéria

Rua de S. Bernardo

Rua do Arco de S. Mamede

Jardim Botânico

4

Tv. do Salitre

1

Jardim da Estrela

Rua de Santo Amaro

Rua da Imprensa Nacional

Rua Prazeres

Rua do Monte Olivete

Tv. Monte do Carmo

Rua de S. Marçal

R. do Jasmim

2

R. da Palmeira Real

R. Conde de Soure

R. Luísa Todi

R. D. Pedro V

Rua das Taipas

CC da Patriarcal

Praça da Alegria

Despite its density, Lisbon's not claustrophobia-inducing, thanks to its spacious squares and peaceful gardens, overflowing with greenery and water features. You can visit many spectacular *miradouros* (viewing points) that make the most of the city's dramatic changes in height. START: **Jardim da Estrela. Tram: 25, 28. Bus: 9, 720, 738, 773.**

1 ★ kids **Jardim da Estrela.** Spacious and leafy, this is a great park to take the smaller kids for a picnic, especially after walking those tough cobbled hills; they may find new verve when they see the toddlers' playpark and a pond full of ducks. *Praça da Estrela.* ☎ 21-397-4818. Free admission. Daily 7am–midnight. Tram: 25, 28. Bus: 9, 720.

2 ★ kids **Jardim do Príncipe Real.** It's surprising what you can fit into such a small space. Even though there's a cafe at both ends, a kids' play area, and an underground water museum (a former waterworks revealing an eerily drippy, subterranean world), it has ample green spaces for a picnic. *Praça do Príncipe Real. Free admission. Open 24 hours. Water Museum*

The tranquil Jardim Botânico.

Admission 2.50€; 1.25€ students, Lisboa Card, seniors; free under 12s. Tues–Sat 10am–6pm Park open 24 hours a day. Bus: 58, 790.

3 ★★ **Parque das Amoreiras.** This small park stands out because of the short section of aqueduct that passes along one side and is decorated with tiled panels. The *amoreiras*, or mulberry trees, once here to supply a nearby silk factory, have long gone, but it's still a pleasantly shady retreat from the summer heat. *See p 74,* **2**.

4 ★★ **Jardim Botânico.** This is a tranquil and shaded oasis with winding paths, small lakes, and benches below towering palms. There's various species of them along with orchids and other tropical plants, and the butterfly house is a spectacular corner of color. *See p 42,* **6**.

5 ★★ **Parque Eduardo VII.** *See p 90.*

6 ★★ **Jardim da Fundação Calouste Gulbenkian.** These grounds have been carefully designed with pathways, various species of tropical and native plants, plus some striking sculptures. I find it the ideal tonic to being 'museumed' out. *Avenida de Berna, 45A.* ☎ 21-782-3000. Tues–Sun 10am–545pm. Metro: São Sebastião/Praça de Espanha. Bus: 16, 26, 31, 46, 56. See also p 16,* **1**.

Parque Florestal **de Monsanto** **& Belém**

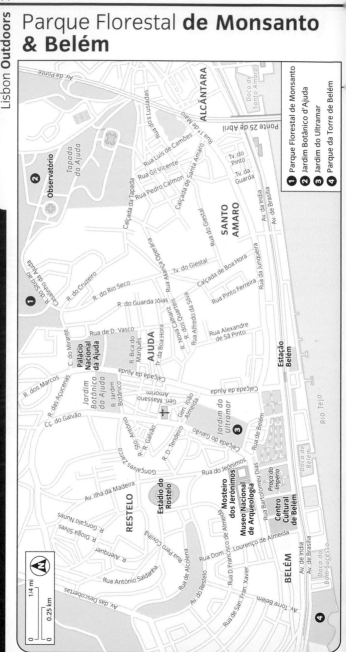

1 Parque Florestal de Monsanto
2 Jardim Botânico d'Ajuda
3 Jardim do Ultramar
4 Parque da Torre de Belém

Wnat I love about west Lisbon is that it has retained its
sense of space with green spots from the vast Parque Florestal de Monsanto to Torre de Belém's shady waterfront park. Stop
for a picnic in the shade, take in the floral scents of tropical gardens,
or opt for something sporty.

**❶ kids Parque Florestal de
Monsanto.** There's no problem
finding something to keep kids
active at these three popular play-
parks. **Pedreira da
Serafina** is a
wooded area with
sheer rock faces,
great for walks and
climbing, while
**Mata de São
Domingos de
Benfica** is an
adventure park
with a climbing
wall. Or you can
bike or roller-blade
along the network of paths and
small roads, play tennis, picnic or
have lunch at a restaurant. In the
north part of the park is the **Palácio
dos Marqueses da Fronteira**,
with the Jardim Zoologico de Lisboa
just beyond it (p 32). *Information
Estrada do Barcal, Monte das
Perdizes.* ☎ 21-817-0200. *Bus: 29
(south), 24 (southeast), 11, 23 (east),
70 (north), 24, 29 (west).*

*Decorative tile at the Palacio dos
Marqueses da Fronteira.*

❷ Jardim Botânico d'Ajuda.
Breathe in the scents of flora, trees,
and flowers from former Portuguese
colonies in Portugal's first botanic
garden. Planted in
1768, it has
retained its Renais-
sance layout with
pathways, lakes,
shaped hedges,
and beds, plus the
later addition of a
baroque fountain
and steps. A sea-
sonal festival of
color, this is definitely
one for keen garden-
ers. *Calçada da Ajuda
s/n.* ☎ *21-362-2503. Admission 2€;
1€ students, seniors; free under 7 &
Sun. Apr daily 9am–7pm; May–Sept
daily 9am–8pm; Oct–Mar daily 9am–
6pm. Tram: 18. Bus: 14, 27, 29, 32.*

❸ Jardim do Ultramar. Tucked
away behind the main restaurant
area and tram stop in Belém, this
beautiful shaded park is home to
the Institute of Tropical Science. Tall

There are relaxing gardens beside the Torre de Belém.

Keen gardeners will enjoy a visit to Jardim Botânico d' Ajuda.

palms line the paths that lead through an Oriental garden, and past tropical trees and plants from former Portuguese colonies. Peacocks strut in and out of the shade near the institute's main building, hopping onto benches to show off their plumes. Look out for ducks too—when I was there, 30-minute-old ducklings were being hustled to safety. *See p 70,* ❶.

❹ **Parque da Torre de Belém.** By the Belém Tower (p 14), this compact park is lush but with plenty of shade and perfect for re-energizing. Just the spot for a picnic, though kids might make a beeline for the adjacent Haagen-Dazs store for an ice cream. Just beyond the park is a monument dedicated to members of Portugal's armed forces who have died in active service. A striking triangular structure, it has at its base a perpetually burning flame. *Avenida de Brasília. Train: Belém. Tram: 15. Bus: 27, 28, 29, 43, 49, 51, 112.* ●

Getting Around Parque Florestal de Monsanto

Monsanto Park is a vast area and somewhat off-putting to the casual visitor who arrives on foot. Pedestrians are most likely to wander the peripheries of the park via the Palacio dos Marqueses da Fronteira (bus 70) on the north side or the Jardim Botânico da Ajuda (bus 14, 73) in the south. For exploring the area further, or for those that want to stay at the campsite here, a car or at least a bicycle is a must. This isn't the kind of green space for gentle afternoon strolls on your own; as sometimes it can feel quite remote (except for the major road passing through it), so you should take at least one other person with you. If in doubt, seek advice from the Information Center here or the Lisbon Welcome Center in the city center.

Dining Best Bets

Best **Wine List**
★★★ Nariz do Vinho Tinto $$ *Rua do Conde (p 107)*

Best for **Families**
★★ Cervejaria Portugália $–$$ *Avenida Brasilia, Ed. Espelho de Agua (p 105)*

Best **Celebrity Chef**
★★★ Manifesto, $$$$, *Largo de Santos (p 107)*

Best **Modern Portuguese**
★★★ Feitoria $$$$$ *Doca de Bom Sucesso (p 106)*

Best **Fish & Seafood**
★★★ Nune's Real Marisqueira. $$$ *Rua Bartolomeu Dias (p 108)*

Best **Slow Food Restaurant**
★★ Santíssimus $$$ *Rua São João da Mata, 33. (p 110)*

Best **Cervejaria (beer hall)**
★★ Cervejaria da Trindade $$ *Rua Nova da Trindade (p 104)*

Best **Budget Dining**
★ Claras em Castelo $. *Rua Bartolomeu Gusmão, 31.(p 106)*

Best for **Cakes & Snacks**
★★★ Antiga Confeitaria de Belém $ *Rua de Belém, 84–92 (p 103)*

Best **Traditional Cafe**
★★ Café Martinho da Arcada $$$ *Praça do Comércio, 3 (p 103)*

Best **Literary Cafe**
★★ A Brasileira $ *Rua Garrett, 120 (p 103)*

Best **Hotel Restaurant**
★★★ Restaurante Ad-Lib $$$–$$$$ *Hotel Sofitel Lisboa, Avenida da Liberdade, 127 (p 109)*

Best **City Views**
★★★ Eleven $$$$$ *Rua Marquês de Fronteira, Jardim Amália Rodrígues (p 103)*

Best for **Special Occasions**
★★★ Gambrinus, $$$$. *Rua das Portas de S Antão, 23. (p 107)*

Best **Award-Winning**
★★★ Restaurante Tavares $$$$$ *Rua da Misericordia (p 111)*

Best **Setting**
★★ Estufa Real $$$ *Calçada do Galvão. (p 106)*

Largo do Carmo.

Alfama Dining

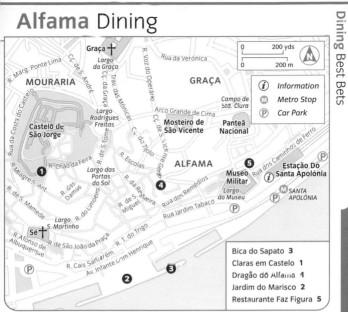

Bica do Sapato **3**
Claras em Castelo **1**
Dragão do Alfama **4**
Jardim do Marisco **2**
Restaurante Faz Figura **5**

Parque das Nações Dining

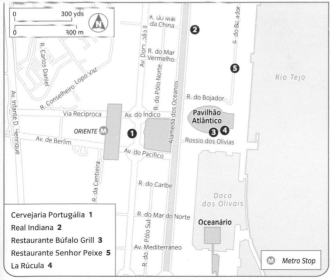

Cervejaria Portugália **1**
Real Indiana **2**
Restaurante Búfalo Grill **3**
Restaurante Senhor Peixe **5**
La Rúcula **4**

City Center Dining

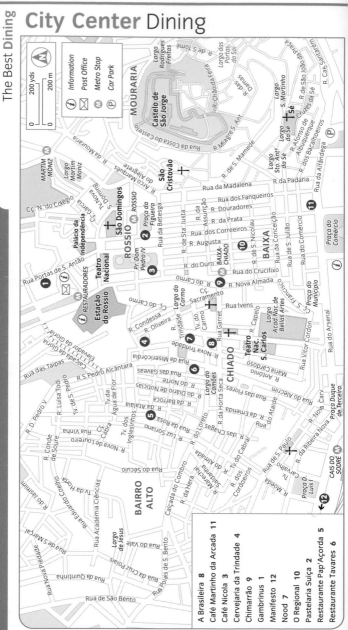

Legend:
- ⓘ Information
- ⊠ Post Office
- Ⓜ Metro Stop
- Ⓟ Car Park

200 yds
200 m

A Brasileira 8
Café Martinho da Arcada 11
Café Nicola 3
Cervejaria da Trindade 4
Chimarrão 9
Gambrinus 1
Manifesto 12
Nood 7
O Regional 10
Pastelaria Suíça 2
Restaurante Pap'Açorda 5
Restaurante Tavares 6

Belém Dining

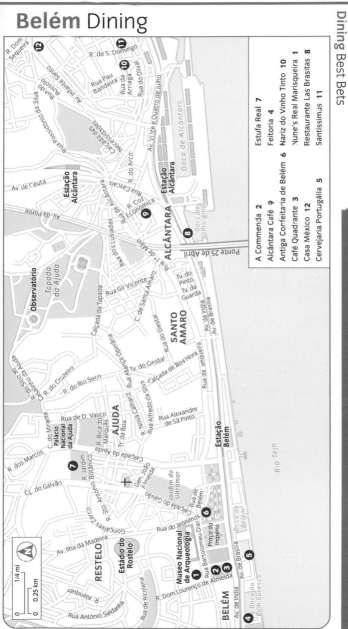

A Commenda **2**
Alcântara Café **9**
Antiga Corfeitaria de Belém **6**
Café Quadrante **3**
Casa México **12**
Cervejaria Portugália **5**
Estufa Real **7**
Feitoria **4**
Nariz do Vinho Tinto **10**
Nune's Real Marisqueira **1**
Restaurante Las Brasitas **8**
Santíssimus **11**

North of City Center Dining

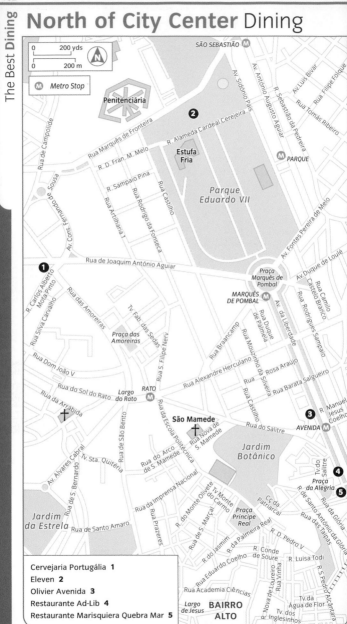

Cervejaria Portugália **1**

Eleven **2**

Olivier Avenida **3**

Restaurante Ad-Lib **4**

Restaurante Marisquiera Quebra Mar **5**

Lisbon **Dining A to Z**

★★ A Brasileira CHIADO *PORTU-GUESE/CAFE* Renowned for the bronze statue of modernist poet Fernando Pessoa outside, this historic cafe doesn't have the politest waiters, but using a few words of Portuguese might help. It has retained interior dark-wood décor and chandeliers, and if you want more than a cake or toasted sandwich, head downstairs for a reasonable Portuguese lunch. *Rua Garrett, 120.* 21-346-9541. *Coffee & cake 3€–4.50€; Entrees 9€–12€. AE, MC, V. Daily; downstairs lunch only. Closed Aug. Tram: 15. Map p 100.*

★★ A Commenda BELEM *MEDI-TERRANEAN* Dine on dishes of fresh tuna with olive dressing or Iberian pork with regional stuffing. As well as occasional themed musical evenings and Sunday buffets, there's a large terrace overlooking the river. *Centro Cultural de Belém, Praça do Império.* 21-361-2610. *Entrees 15€–25€. AE, MC, V. Lunch & dinner daily, lunch only Sun. Tram: 15. Map p 101.*

★★ Alcântara Café ALCANTARA *MODERN PORTUGUESE* Combining modern industrial décor, gilt-edged mirrors, and a large Hellenistic statue of Vitória de Samutrácia, this warehouse restaurant aims to be a 'modern classic', with inventive Portuguese cuisine. Reservations advised. *Rua Maria Luísa Holstein 15.* 21-363-7176. *Entrees 20€–38€. AE, MC, V. Dinner daily. Tram: 12. Map p 101.*

★★★ Antiga Confeitaria de Belém BELEM *CAFE* Dating back to 1837 and firmly on the tourist trail, this historic cafe won't disappoint. Either go local and order *um café* (small black coffee) and a *pastel*, their famed custard tart, at the

Statue of writer Fernando Pessoa outside the Café A Brasileira.

front counter, or go into the warren of tile-clad back rooms for waiter service. *Rua de Belém, 84–92.* 21-363-7423. *Coffee/tea & pastel 1.50€–3€. Daily. Tram: 15. Map p 101.*

★★★ Bica do Sapato ALFAMA *PORTUGUESE* Whether you choose the cafe for seafood rice and duck pie, or the pricier restaurant for beef tornedo, stuffed rabbit, and roast turbot, this renowned restaurant is about quality. There's also a decent sushi bar and vegetarian options available in the restaurant. *Avenida Dom Henrique, Arm. B, Cais da Pedra.* 21-881-320. *Entrees 12€–32€. AE, MC, V. Restaurant lunch & dinner Tues–Sat, dinner only Mon; Cafeteria lunch & dinner, snacks & dinner only Mon; sushi bar dinner Mon–Sat. Bus: 6, 12, 34. Map p 99.*

★★ Café Martinho da Arcada BAIXA *PORTUGUESE/CAFE* Lisbon's

Antiga Confeitaria de Belém.

oldest cafe, first founded in 1778, was another haunt of the poet Fernando Pessoa and you'll see a table still laid for him in the restaurant. Dine on their house-styled *bacalhau* (cod) or tender baked goat, or just stop for a coffee in the attractive cafe. *Praça do Comércio, 3.* ☎ *21-886-6213. Coffee & cake 2€–5€. Entrees 15€–20€. AE, DC, MC, V. Lunch & dinner, Mon–Sat. Tram: 15, 25, 28. Metro: Baixa-Chaido. Map p 100.*

★ **Café Nicola** BAIXA *CAFE* Another historic cafe once frequented by Lisbon intellectuals, with a modernist façade facing onto Rossio Square. Stand at the counter for a quick coffee. If you sit down you'll pay double or more. *Praça Dom Pedro IV.* ☎ *21-346 0579. Coffee & cake 2.50€–5€, Mon–Sat. Closed Sun. Metro: Rossio. Tram: 15. Map p 100.*

★ **Café Quadrante** BELEM *INTERNATIONAL* The Belém Cultural Center's self-service restaurant is a good option for quick lunches and early dinners, offering quiche and salad, soup or pasta. *Avenida Brasília, Ed. Apoio á Naútico.* ☎ *21-362-0865. Centro Cultural de Belém, Praça do Imperio.* ☎ *21-362-9256. Entrees 8€–12€. AE, MC, V. Lunch & dinner daily. Tram: 15. Map p 101.*

★★ **Casa México** ALCANTARA *MEXICAN* Expect the usual Mexican enchiladas and nachos plus a tasty surprise starter of battered pork and strawberry sauce dip. The jugs of sangria are well prepared and décor is bright and fun. *Avenida Dom Carlos I.* ☎ *21-397-4790. Entrees 10€–16€. AE, MC, V. Lunch Mon–Fri, dinner Sat & Sun. Tram: 12, 15. Map p 101.*

★★ **Cervejaria da Trindade** BAIRRO ALTO *PORTUGUESE* Covered in Portuguese tiles, this is a relaxed and comfortable beer hall and restaurant housed in a former monastery refectory. Try the crab served on a wooden board with a hammer and a glass of beer. *Rua Nova da Trindade.* ☎ *21-342-3506. Entrees 12€–17€. AE, DC, MC, V.*

Lunch & dinner daily. Closed public holidays. Elevador da Gloria. Metro: Restauradores. Map p 100.

★ kids **Cervejaria Portugália**
BELEM *PORTUGUESE* This reliable chain of restaurants (some in shopping centers) serves affordable Portuguese cuisine, including steaks in gravy topped with ham and egg, a range of prawn dishes, and a kids' menu. *Avenida Brasilia, Ed. Espelho de Agua.* ☎ 21-303-2700. Entrees 8€–13€. AE, MC, V. Lunch & dinner daily. Tram: 15. Map p 101.

Amoreiras Shopping. ☎ 21-384-4796. Entrees 8€–13€. AE, MC, V. Lunch & dinner daily. Metro: Rato.

Centro Comercial Vasco da Gama. ☎ 21-011-482. Entrees 8€–13€. AE, MC, V. Lunch & dinner daily. Metro: Oriente.

★ kids **Chimarrão** CHIADO *BRAZILIAN* A popular shopping center restaurant, this is a Brazilian-style *rodizio* (grill) with various all-you-can-eat options. Pile your plate high with salad, chips, rice, and stacks of meat. Some offers also include a drink and dessert. *Rua do Carmo, Armazens do Chiado.* ☎ 21-347-9444. All you can eat menu from 8€.

Enjoy a platter of oysters in Cervejaria da Trindade.

AE, MC, V. Lunch & dinner daily. Metro: Baixa-Chiado. Map p 100.

Alameda dos Oceanos, Parque das Nações. ☎ 21-895-2222. All you can eat menu from 8€. AE, MC, V. Lunch & dinner daily. Metro: Oriente.

Amoreiras Shopping. ☎ 21-386-2363. All you can eat menu from 8€. AE, MC, V. Lunch & dinner daily. Metro: Rato.

Café Martinho da Arcada.

The Michelin-starred Eleven has fantastic views across the city.

★ **Claras em Castelo** ALFAMA *PORTUGUESE* This tiny, pastel-pink eatery at the castle gate is a good-value lunchtime pit stop. Enjoy fresh salmon, squid and tuna salads, homemade vegetable soup, hot plates of bacalhau, and a glass of house white. *Rua Bartolomeu Gusmão, 31. Entrees 5€–7.50€. Lunch and early dinner daily. Tram: 28. Bus: 37. Map p 99.*

★ **Dragão do Alfama** ALFAMA *PORTUGUESE* A small eatery with typical blue and white tiles and photos of famous *fado* singers on the walls, with live *fado* on Thursday, Friday, and Saturday evenings. The menu includes grilled squid and prawns and oven-baked *bacalhau*. *Rua Guillerme Braga, 8.* ☎ *21-886-777. Entrees 12€–15€. AE, MC, V. Dinner Mon–Sat. Tram: 28. Map p 99.*

★★★ **Eleven** AVENIDA/PARQUE *MODERN PORTUGUESE* Lisbon's first Michelin-starred restaurant, Eleven is tastefully styled with contemporary art complementing fantastic views across the city. Choose from the lunchtime business menu or a five-course tasting menu. *Rua Marquês de Fronteira, Jardim Amália Rodrígues.* ☎ *21-386-2211. Lunch Business menu 39€; tasting menu 79€. AE, DC, MC, V. Lunch & dinner Tues–Sat. Closed public holidays. Metro: Parque. Map p 102.*

★★ **Estufa Real** BELEM *PORTUGUESE* Escape the crowds at this restaurant set in the former Royal Greenhouse at the Jardim Botânico d'Ajuda (p 95). An oasis of calm, it has a dining room and lounge overlooking the lush gardens. Come for Sunday brunch of scrambled eggs, smoked fish, meats, and even oysters, or carefully prepared lunches of bacalhau, partridge, or beef fillet. *Calçada do Galvão.* ☎ *21-361-9400. Entrees 16.50€–22€. AE, MC, V. Lunch only. Tram: 15. Map p 101.*

★★★ **Feitoria** BELEM *PORTUGUESE* Chef José Cordeiro is being marked out as one to watch in terms of innovative modern Portuguese cuisine. Having gained a Michelin star while working at Casa Calçada (Amarante), he now heads up Altis Belem's new hotel restaurant, using the discoveries theme to create dishes that are both visually spectacular and taste sensations. *Altis Belem, Doca de Bom Sucesso.* ☎ *21-040-0200. 4-course tasting* menu 40€, five-course 50€, entrees 21€–26€. AE, DC, MC, V. Lunch & dinner daily. Tram: 15. Map p 101.

★★★ Gambrinus BAIXA PORTU-GUESE/FISH

One of the city's most acclaimed restaurants, with a history dating back decades and a clientele that includes politicians and celebrities. It doesn't come cheap so book ahead and plan on a big night out. *Rua das Portas de S Antão, 23.* ☎ 21-342-1466. *Entrees 28€–36€. AE, DC, MC, V. Lunch & dinner daily. Metro: Rossio, Restauradores. Map p 100.*

★★ Jardim do Marisco ALFAMA

PORTUGUESE/FISH In a large warehouse on the waterfront, and a good choice for a varied menu of fresh fish, as well as regional meat dishes. Try the seafood platter for two or specialties like grouper macaroni. *Jardim do Tabaco, Avenida Dom Henrique.* ☎ 21-882-4240. *Entrees 10€–16€; AE, DC, MC, V. Lunch & dinner Tues–Sat; dinner only Mon. Closed Aug. Bus: 9, 28, 35. Map p 99.*

★★ La Rúcula PARQUE NACOES

ITALIAN This modern Italian restaurant has views of the river and Pavilhão Atlântico. Choose from a selection of pizzas, pasta, and steaks, followed by sweet Italian desserts such as tiramisu. *Rossio dos Olivais.* ☎ 21-892-2747. *Entrees 12€–18€; AE, DC, MC, V. Lunch & dinner daily. Metro: Oriente. Map p 99.*

★★★ Manifesto SANTOS PORTU-GUESE

Although he has been around for several years, experienced Luis Baena is one of Lisbon's most talked-about chefs of the moment. The restaurant's Pop Art décor is as bold as the gourmet menu, which focuses on local, natural produce and creatively presented plates. *Largo de Santos, 2.* ☎ 21-396-3419. *Entrees 18€–25€. AE, MC, V. Lunch & dinner. Closed Sun. Tram: 15. Map p 100.*

★★★ Nariz do Vinho Tinto

ALCANTARA PORTUGUESE This traditional restaurant is popular with families, offering up dishes of prosunto (cured ham), Portuguese

Restaurante Olivier Avenida.

Stylish hotel restaurant Ad-Lib.

cheeses, fried sole with banana, or roast duck with honey. *Rua do Conde.* ☎ 21-395-035. *Entrees 12.50€–30€. AE, MC, DC, V. Lunch & dinner Tues–Fri; dinner only Sat. Tram: 15, 2.5. Map p 101.*

★ **Nood** CHIADO *ASIAN* A chain of restaurants offering fast, tasty, and reasonably priced Asian food. Starters include the likes of meat filled pan-fried dumplings, while mains comprise big bowls of noodle soup with meat or fish, or chicken *katsu* curry and various other rice or noodle dishes. *Largo Rafael Bordeiro, 2.* ☎ 21-347-4747 *Entrees 7.25€–9.90€. AE, MC, V. Lunch & dinner. Closed Sun. Metro: Restauradores. Elevador da Glória. Map p 100.*

★★ **Nune's Real Marisqueira** BELEM *PORTUGUESE/FISH* One of the best-known fish restaurants in the city, this relaxed venue serves up fresh shellfish alongside grouper, salmon, and turbot. There's meat too, mostly steaks and skewers, but fish is definitely the order of the day. *Rua Bartolomeu Dias.* ☎ 21-301-9899. *Entrees 12.50€–25€. AE, MC, V. Lunch & dinner Mon–Sun. Closed Wed. Tram: 15. Map p 101.*

★★ **Olivier Avenida** CHIADO *MODERN FRENCH/PORTUGUESE* Although the restaurant has become somewhat consumed by its own reputation as a beautiful people's hangout, chef Olivier Costa's menu is no wilting wallflower. Starters include octopus carpaccio and game sausage, and main courses lobster risotto or mini hamburgers with foie gras. Wine prices certainly fit the affluent clientele, some topping the 1000€ mark. *Hotel Tivoli Jardim, Rua Julia Cesar Machado, 7.* ☎ 21-317-4105. *Tasting menu 36€. AE, DC, MC, V. Dinner only. Closed Sun. Tram: 28, Elevador da Glória. Metro: Rossio. Map p 102. Rua do Alecrim, 23.* ☎ 21-342-2916. *Tram: 28. Metro: Baixa-Chiado.*

★ **O Regional** BAIXA *PORTUGUESE* Right in the heart of the Baixa, this unassuming restaurant is not on the tourist trail. The menu comprises authentic Portuguese cuisine such as house-style *bacalhau*, skewered fish, or spit-roast meat, with old-fashioned homemade desserts like *arroz doce* (rice pudding) and thick chocolate mousse. *Rua dos Sapateiros.* ☎ 21-342-1027. *Entrees 10€–15€. AE, DC, MC, V. Lunch &*

dinner daily. Metro: Baixa-Chiado. Map p 100.

★★ Pastelaria Suiça BAIXA *POR-TUGUESE/CAFE*   This huge and historic cafe straddles both Rossio and Figueira squares, so you can sit in either one. Choose from the wide range of sinful-looking cakes and pastries. *Praça Dom Pedro IV.* ☎ *21-321-4090. Coffee & cake 2.50€–4.50€. AE, MC, V. Daily. Metro: Rossio. Tram: 15. Map p 100.*

★ Real Indiana PARQUE NACOES *INDIAN*   A good choice in vegetarian fare, along with the usual meat and seafood favorites including starters of chicken samosa and prawn puri, and for mains there's chicken tikka masala and lamb madras. *Alameda dos Oceanos.* ☎ *21-896-0303. Entrees 7.50€–21€. AE, DC, MC, V. Lunch & dinner daily. Metro: Oriente. Map p 99.*

★★★ Restaurante Ad-Lib AVE-NIDA *MODERN MEDITERRANEAN*

A stylish hotel restaurant with sleek, black tables, autumnal gold and orange décor, and original works of art. The food lives up to the setting: *bacalhau*, ravioli, prawns with garlic, coriander and a chouriço emulsion, or medallions of veal, with matched wines. *Hotel Sofitel Lisboa, Avenida da Liberdade, 127.* ☎ *21-322-8350. Entrees 19€–28€. AE, DC, MC, V. Lunch & dinner daily. Metro: Avenida. Map p 102.*

★★ Restaurante Búfalo Grill PARQUE NACOES *BRAZILIAN*   A favorite Brazilian *rodizio* (grill) in Lisbon, you'll need plenty of space for all-you-can-eat deals, although you can opt for the smaller version. Meal deals can include a cold buffet, Brazilian black beans, fried banana, rice, and liberal slices of meat from steaming skewers. *Rossio dos Olivais, Parque das Nações.* ☎ *21-892-2740. Buffet menu 7.95€–17.95€. AE, DC, MC, V. Lunch & dinner daily. Metro: Oriente. Map p 99.*

Restaurante Búfalo Grill.

★★ Restaurante Faz Figura

ALFAMA *MODERN PORTUGUESE* This venue is aiming for modern Portuguese but actually offers a fairly traditional menu, including oven-cooked baby goat and stuffed squid. What makes it special are the views over the river, relaxed ambiance, and a decent selection of regional wines. *Rua do Paraíso, 15B.* ☎ *21-886-8981. Entrees 15€–23€. AE, MC, V. Lunch & dinner. Tram: 28. Map p 99.*

★★ Restaurante Las Brasitas

ALCANTARA *PORTUGUESE* This is one for the meat lovers with Argentinian-inspired steaks—not quite as large as the Latin American version. There are also fish options, including Mozambique prawn skewers and fresh grilled salmon. *Doca de Santo Amaro, Arm. 16.* ☎ *21-396-0647. Entrees 9.50€–29.50€. AE, MC, V. Lunch & dinner. Tram: 15. Map p 101.*

★★ Restaurante Marisquiera Quebra Mar

AVENIDA *PORTUGUESE/FISH* Either come here early or book ahead for this popular fish restaurant. You'll see displays of fish in the window and the menu is no less impressive, with everything from octopus salad and mixed fish grill to *bacalhau minhota* (salted cod with garlic, cabbage and potatoes—a traditional Christmas dish). *Avenida da Liberdade, 77.* ☎ *21-346-4855. Entrees 15€–22€. AE, DC, MC, V. Lunch & dinner. Metro: Avenida. Map p 102.*

★★★ Restaurante Pap'Açorda

CHIADO *PORTUGUESE* This restaurant has been one of the classic 'must-try' places in Lisbon for many years, which means they're always pressed for time and space. Now it's gaining a reputation for its grumpy waiters, but it still serves up pricey Portuguese cuisine. The menu is traditional featuring lobster and prawns, grouper, ribs, and baby goat. *Rua da Atalaia.* ☎ *21-346-4811. Entrees 16€–40€. AE, DC, MC, V. Lunch & dinner. Closed Sun & Mon. Metro: Baixa-Chiado Map p 100.*

★★ Restaurante Senhor Peixe

PARQUE NACOES *PORTUGUESE/FISH* Smaller than many of the restaurants along this 'strip', the fish certainly makes it a popular choice, with turbot and a good-value fish of the day. *Rua da Pimenta.* ☎ *21-895-5892. Entrees 12€–45€. AE, DC, MC, V. Lunch & dinner. Closed Mon. Metro: Oriente. Map p 99.*

★★★ Restaurante Tavares

BAIRRO ALTO *INTERNATIONAL* Lisbon's oldest restaurant and renowned for its popularity with Portuguese writers such as Eça de Queiros. It doesn't come cheap, but it always employs the best chefs; José Avillez, chef at the time of writing, was awarded a Michelin star at the end of 2009. You're greeted by a uniformed doorman and dine in a palatial room with glass chandeliers. *Rua da Misericordia.* ☎ *21-342-1112. Entrees 45€–60€. Tasting menu 65€. AE, DC, MC, V. Dinner. Tram: 28. Map p 100.*

★★★ Santissimus

SANTOS *PORTUGUESE/EUROPEAN* The concept here is 'slow food', but you're always well attended by the one waiter, who seems to juggle tables with expert precision. Warm, flavored rolls keep you going until the next course, starters are savory bites sufficient for two, and main courses and desserts are twists on classical European cuisine, from roast lamb to risotto and fruit crumble. *Rua São João da Mata, 33.* ☎ *914-328-161. Entrees 11.25€–14€. AE, DC, MC, V. Lunch & dinner. Closed Mon. Tram: 25. Map p 101.* ●

The Best **Nightlife**

Nightlife Best Bets

Best Place for Ginjinhas
★ Ginjinha do Rossio, *Largo São Domingos (p 116)*

Best Place for Port Lovers
★★★ Solar do Vinho do Porto, *Rua de São Pedro de Alcântara, 45 (p 122)*

Best Place for Fado
★★★ Clube de Fado, *Rua São João da Praça, 94 (p 119)*

Best Place for Cocktails
★ Cinco Lounge, *Rua Rubén A Leitao. (p 118)*

Best Gay Disco & Bar
★★ Trumps, *Rua da Imprensa Nacional, 104B (p 120)*

Best Student Bar
★ Mezcal, *Travessa da Agua da Flor, 20 (p 117)*

Best Irish Pub
Hennessey's Irish Pub, *Rua do Cais do Sodré, 32–38 (p 117)*

Best Place for Dance Music
★★ Lux, *Avenida Dom Henrique (p 119)*

Best Place for Jazz
★★ Hot Clube de Portugal, *Rua da Alegría, 39 (p 121)*

Best Terrace Bar
★★ O Terraço, *Calçada do Marques de Tancos, 3, (p 117)*

Best Wine Bar
★★ Enoteca de Belém, *Rua do Marta Pinto, 10/1, (p 122)*

Find taxi ranks at the major squares.

Alcântara/Belém Nightlife

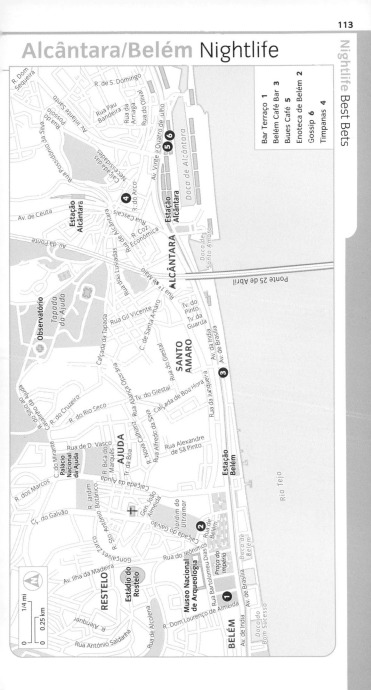

Bar Terraço **1**
Belém Café Bar **3**
Blues Café **5**
Enoteca de Belém **2**
Gossip **6**
Timpanas **4**

City Center Nightlife

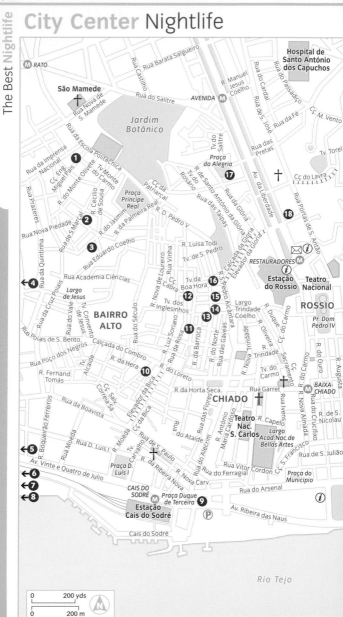

Adega Mesquita **13**

Bar 106 **2**

Café Luso **14**

Casino do Estoril **6**

Catacumbas Jazz Bar **12**

Cinco Lounge **3**

Club Souk **10**

Clube de Fado **21**

Dragão do Alfama **24**

Frágil **11**

Ginjinha do Rossio **19**

Hard Rock Café **18**

Hennessy's Irish Pub **9**

Hot Clube de Portugal **17**

Incognito Bar **4**

The Loft **5**

Lux Bar (& Club) **25**

Mezcal **15**

O Terraço **20**

Onda Jazz **22**

Op Art Café **7**

Solar do Vinho do Porto **16**

Speakeasy Bar **8**

Taverna d'El Rey **23**

Trumps **1**

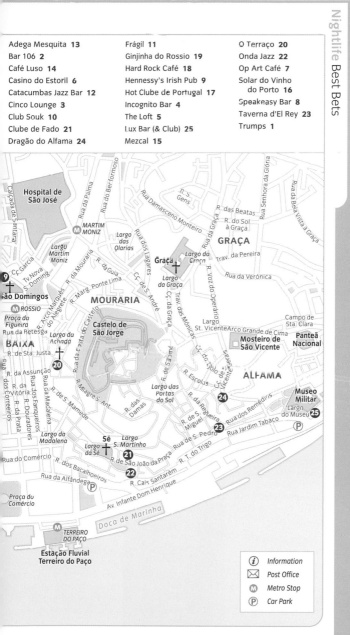

Information

Post Office

Metro Stop

Car Park

Parque das Nações Nightlife

0 — 300 yds
0 — 300 m

Av. do Atlântico

R. do Mar da China

R. do Mar Vermelho

Av. Dom João II

R. do Pólo Norte

R. do Bojador ❶

❷

Rio Tejo

R. Carlos Daniel

R. Mário Viegas

R. Conselheiro Lopo Vaz

Av. Infante D. Henrique

Via Recíproca

Av. do Índico

Alameda dos Oceanos

R. do Bojador

Pavilhão Atlântico

ORIENTE Ⓜ

Av. de Berlim

Av. do Pacífico

Rossio dos Olivais

R. da Centieira

R. do Caribe

❸

Doca dos Olivais

R. do Mar do Norte

Oceanário

Av. do Báltico

R. do Pólo Sul

Av. Mediterrâneo

Casino Lisboa **3**
Irish & Co **1**
Peter Café Sport **2**

Av. de Ulisses

Ⓜ Metro Stop

Lisbon Nightlife A to Z

Bars & Pubs

★ **Bar Terraço** BELEM   Located inside the CCB, this is the place for a quiet drink, light bites, and gentle background music. At night take in the view across the illuminated Tagus River. *Centro Cultural de Belém,* ☎ *21-362-0865. Tram: 15. Map p 113.*

★★ **Belém Café Bar** BELEM   A large venue featuring a lounge bar with candles, sofas, and mirrors beside a restaurant offering unspoiled views of

Irish & Co.

the 25 de Abril Bridge and the Cristo Rei statue opposite. During the week there's an ambient soundtrack but on Saturday nights it's a livelier scene with DJs playing the latest dance tunes. During the summer an outdoor bar and dancefloor open up. *Avenida Brasília – Pavilhão Poente.* ☎ *21-362-4232. Tram: 15. Map p 113.*

★★ **Ginjinha do Rossio** BAIXA   This hole-in-the wall bar just off Rossio Square is a regular stop-off for people of all ages and walks of life. It only

Try traditional cherry brandy in Ginjinha do Rossio.

serves ginjinha, cherry brandy served in small plastic cups for 1.20€ a shot. *Largo São Domingos, 8. Metro: Rossio. Map p 114.*

★★ Hennessy's Irish Pub CAIS DO SODRE   Popular with both Irish and Brits, this screens major sport matches and has regular live music. The inside of the bar is decorated with themed bric-à-brac and it serves everything from Guinness to Bailey's matched by a mixed menu. *Rua do Cais do Sodré, 32–38. ☎ 21-347-6988. Tram: 15, 25. Metro: Cais do Sodré. Map p 114.*

★★ Irish & Co PARQUE DAS NACOES   Part of a chain, it tries hard to be an authentic Irish pub but it's a little too clinical. Fine for a decent pint of Guinness or Kilkenny and a stout pie though. *Rua da Pimenta, 57–61. ☎ 21-894-0558. Metro: Oriente. Map p 116.*

★★ Mezcal BAIRRO ALTO   A Mexican-style bar with music and drink to match. During term time, you'll hear every European language being spoken here, as it's a favorite spot with Erasmus exchange students in Lisbon for one or two semesters. By the end of the night, and after too many tequilas, it can get a bit squalid. *Travessa da Agua da Flor, 20. ☎ 21-343-1863. Tram: 28. Map p 114.*

★★ O Terraço ALFAMA   Located on the site of a former market, this bar is about as laid back as you'll get. Mix 'n' match sofas, deckchairs, and beanbags are dotted across a terrace with unbeatable views over the city. It's perfect for cooling off on a summer evening with a sundowner cocktail, There's also shade if you need it, or if you happen to be here when it's cooler, you can grab a blanket. *Calçada do Marques de Tancos, 3. ☎ 21-353-0181. Tram: 28. Map p 114.*

★★ Peter Café Sport PARQUE DAS NACOES   The original gin palace and restaurant opened in the Azores in 1918 and remains a favorite stop-off for sailors crossing the Atlantic. Still run by the same family, they opened this venue a few years ago, where you can relax on the terrace with a G&T. *Avenida do Borador X. Metro: Oriente. Map p 116.*

Casinos

★★ Casino do Estoril   *See p 114.*

Casino Lisboa PARQUE DAS NACOES   This modern casino in Nations' Park is nearer to the city center than the one in Estoril (p 116). The gambling rooms include black jack and poker, plus there's a lounge bar, live music, restaurants, and glamorous shows. Remember to dress smartly and take some ID. *Alameda dos Oceanos.* ☎ *21-466-7700. Metro: Oriente. Map p 116.*

Cocktail Bars

★ **Cinco Lounge** BAIRRO ALTO Tucked away behind Jardim do Principe Real, this fashion-conscious bar is run by English couple Dave and Julie. This is the place to come for cocktails and their huge menu is impressive. Sip drinks from around the world or try favorites from yesteryear like gin fizz, Long Island iced tea, and martini as well as non-alcoholic mocktails and the house specials with fresh fruit. *Rua Rubén A Leitao.* ☎ *21-342-4033. Funicular da Glória. Metro: Restauradores. Map p 114.*

★★ **Op Art Café** ALCANTARA   A cafe and restaurant by day, Op Art transforms into a late-night dance venue. Its funky décor of geometrical designs, long cocktail list, enviable riverside location almost touching 25 de Abril Bridge, and guest DJs means it has no problem attracting hordes of dance music fans looking for a late night out. *Doca de Santo Amaro.* ☎ *21-395-6787. Tram: 15. Map p 114.*

Dance Clubs

★★ **Blues Café** ALCANTARA Popular for its restaurant with a modern international menu, but from 2am the Blues Café's classy club takes over with a mix of jazz, blues, and dance sounds. Spread over four floors, you can relax with friends in a retro-modern atmosphere with large red lightshades, fringed table lamps, and potted palms. *Rua Cintura Porto, Armazen H.* ☎ *21-395-7085. Tram: 15. Map p 113.*

★★ **Club Souk** WATERFRONT An 'underground micro club', Club Souk hosts club nights with DJs mixing a fusion of global sounds and dance tunes. It also doubles up as a gallery with work by local artists on display. *Rua Marechal Saldanha, 6.* ☎ *21-346-5859. Tram: 28. Metro: Baixa-Chiado. Map p 114.*

★★ **Frágil** BAIRRO ALTO   This veteran club-bar continuously stays at the top of its game by evolving with contemporary culture. You can expect to hear a mix of drum 'n' bass, reggae, and samba in a down-to-earth atmosphere. It also hosts everything from poetry to video events. *Rua da Atalaia, 126.* ☎ *21-346-9578. Tram: 28. Map p 114.*

Check out the four floors at the Blues Café.

Lux Bar is Lisbon's most famous clubbing venue.

★★ **The Loft** ALCANTARA This club combines the industrial look with neon lighting in pinks and blues, metallic and glass bar areas, soft seating, and large dance floors. From Thursday to Saturday the floor fills with people bobbing to dance tunes until the early hours. *Rua do Instituto Industrial.* ☎ 21-396-4841. *Tram: 15. Map p 114.*

★★ **Lux Bar (& Club)** APOLONIA This is Lisbon's most famous club, a legendary dance, drum 'n' bass, hip-hop club that pulls in the punters for top DJs. Dress to impress or come early to avoid long lines and ridiculous entrance charges that will leave your wallet empty. Inside, it's everything you'd expect from a top club with stylish décor, sofas to lounge on, and chandeliers. *Avenida Dom Henrique.* ☎ 21-840-4977. *Bus: 6, 12, 24. Map p 114.*

Fado

Adega Mesquita BAIRRO ALTO A *fado* house with a long tradition of live performances, this is a popular

choice for enjoying traditional Portuguese food as well as the *fado* itself. Music from 8pm onwards. *Rua Diário de Notícias, 107.* ☎ 21-321-9280. *Dinner & show 35€–50€. Tram: 28. Map p 114.*

Café Luso BAIRRO ALTO A veteran *fado* Portuguese restaurant, dating back to 1927, in the basement of a former palace, with a nightly folkloric dance group in traditional dress, followed by live *fado.* After 1am you can come just to listen to the music. The bill can stack up though as they tend to charge for every piece of bread. *Travessa da Queimada, 10.* ☎ 21-342-2281. *Dinner & show 50€–65€; drink & show 30€. Metro: Baixa-Chiado. Map p 114.*

★★ **Clube de Fado** ALFAMA Owned by *fado* guitarist Mario Pachecho and located behind the cathedral, this is a quality venue with performances during dinner and a traditional Portuguese menu. It's not cheap but worth it at least once, and Mario usually performs

Catch traditional folk dancing and fado at Café Luso.

himself. *Rua São João da Praça, 94.* ☎ *21-885-2704. Dinner & show 50€–70€; Tram: 28. Map p 114.*

★★ **Dragão do Alfama** ALFAMA Located in the heart of the Alfama, this is a restaurant with live *fado* music on Thursday, Friday, and Saturday. A far cry from the venues aimed at the tourists; Teresa Salgueiro, a singer with Madredeus, was reputedly 'discovered' here. *Rua Guillerme Braga, 8.* ☎ *21-886-777. Entrees 8€–12€. Tram: 28. Map p 114.*

Taverna d'El Rey BAIRRO ALTO This rustic Alfama house was opened by *fadista* Maria Jô Jô four decades ago. Today you can still enjoy her melancholic voice and enjoy a traditional Portuguese menu. *Largo do Chafariz de Dentro, 15.* ☎ *21-887-6754. Dinner & show 30€–55€. Tram: 28. Map p 114.*

Timpanas ALCANTARA This *fado* house has been entertaining visitors since 1963. The menu is a mixture of Portuguese and Mediterranean cuisine and there are folkloric and *fado* performances nightly. *Rua Gilberto Rola, 24.* ☎ *21-390-6555.*

Dinner & show 45€–60€; drink & show 35€. Tram: 15. Map p 113.

Gay & Lesbian Bars/Clubs

★★ **Bar 106** BAIRRO ALTO A popular international gay bar providing a safe and comfortable night out. Now entering its third decade, it also hosts parties and theme nights. *Rua de São Marçal, 106.* ☎ *21-342-7373. Tram: 28. Metro: Baixa-Chiado. Map p 114.*

★★ **Gossip** ALCANTARA Formerly known as Queens, this is Lisbon's largest gay club, located by the renovated Alcântara docks in a huge warehouse, with a bright neon front. It's large, loud, and brash with plenty of flashing lights, attracting a mixed crowd for all-night house music. There's also an outdoor terrace and bar, where you can cool off. *Rua de Cintura do Porto, Armazen H.* ☎ *21-395-5870. Tram: 15. Map p 113.*

Trumps BAIRRO ALTO/RATO Lisbon's trendiest gay venue, Trumps has a cafe, bars, and a dance club spread over two floors. The décor is a mixture of metal, glitter, and neon lighting downstairs; black floors and trendy chandeliers upstairs. The music is pop/house, plus there are regular shows with everything from flame throwers to drag acts. *Rua da Imprensa Nacional, 104B.* ☎ *21-397-1059. Metro: Rato. Map p 114.*

Jazz Bars

★★ Catacumbas Jazz Bar

BAIRRO ALTO   On a street renowned for its trendy bars, and a good alternative to the expensive *fado* nights in other parts of the Bairro Alto. You'll find a younger crowd here as well as former students of the Hot Clube de Portugal school performing jazz and blues. *Travesia Agua da Flor, 43.* ☎ *21-346-3969. Tram: 28. Map p 114.*

★★ Hot Clube de Portugal

AVENIDA   Portugal's first 'jazz cave', this club is linked to the jazz school next door. Some of Portugal's best jazz musicians have started out here, so it's a good place to catch a few up-and-coming stars. *Rua da Alegria, 39.* ☎ *21-361-8740. Metro: Avenida. Map p 114.*

★★ Onda Jazz ALFAMA   Located

in a small street opposite the Clube de Fado, this is a veritable jazz 'cave'. You can dine here on Portuguese classics, but the main draw is

Dancers at Trumps.

the music, with live acts every week. *Arco de Jesus, 7.* ☎ *21-888-3242. Metro: Cais do Sodré. Map p 114.*

★★ Speakeasy Bar ALCANTARA

This large bar-restaurant has a relaxed feel, with bare brick walls plastered with images of musicians and singers. Although jazz is

The relaxed Speakeasy Bar.

regularly on the agenda, you can also expect to hear anything from rock to *fado*, so check in advance to make sure it's to your taste. *Cais das Oficinas, Armazen 115.* ☎ *21-390-9166.Tram: 15. Map p 114.*

Rock/Alternative Venues

★★ **Hard Rock Café** AVENIDA It might not be particularly 'alternative' but the Hard Rock Café certainly caters to the rock fan. Expect the usual merchandise, guitars on the walls, and classic rock tunes with large video screens. They also do a good line in burgers, ribs, and potent cocktails, and these days it's no more expensive than most middle-range restaurant-bars. *Avenida da Liberdade, 2.* ☎ *21-324-5280. Metro: Restauradores. Map p 114.*

★★ **Incognito Bar** BAIRRO ALTO You'll have to be pretty clued-up to go to this cool underground spot, and that's just to find the right door as it's unmarked. Located on two levels, there's indie, electronica, and techno music on different nights. *Rua Poiais de São Bento, 37.* ☎ *21-390-8755. Tram: 28. Map p 114.*

Wine (& Port) Bars

★★ **Enoteca de Belém** BELEM Reopened in 2009 under new management, this is one of Portugal's new breed of wine bars. It's a good place to sample the country's regional wines by the glass or by the carafe. If you're not sure what to choose, staff will pick out wines according to your taste. *Rua do Marta Pinto, 10/12. Tram: 15. Map p 113.*

★★★ **Solar do Vinho do Porto** BAIRRO ALTO This gently sophisticated bar is the perfect place to relax at the end of a day's sightseeing. Sink into a comfortable sofa and try a few port wines, which can range hugely in price. You don't have to spend a fortune to get something palatable though, and you can accompany it with a plate of bread and cheeses. *Rua de São Pedro de Alcântara, 45.* ☎ *21-347-5707. Daily. Metro: Restauradores. Map p 114.* ●

Arts & Entertainment
Best Bets

Best **Concert Acoustics**
★★★ Fundação Calouste Gulbenkian, *Avenida da Berna (p 127)*

Best **Opera House**
★★★ Teatro Nacional de São Carlos, *Rua de Serpa Pinto, 9 (p 127)*

Best for **Contemporary Performance Arts**
★★★ Centro Cultural de Belém, *Praça do Império (p 127)*

Best **Ballet Venue**
★★ Teatro Camões, *Paseo Neptuno (p 128)*

Best **Sporting Event**
★★★ SL Benfica, *Avenida Lusiada (p 129)*

Best **Theater Performances**
★★★ Teatro Nacional de Dona Maria II, *Praça Dom Pedro IV (p 130)*

Best **Place for Musicals**
★★ Coliseu dos Recreios, *Rua das Portas de Santo Antão (p 127)*

Best **Place for Major Concerts**
★★★ Pavilhão Atlântico, *Rossio dos Olivais (p 127)*

Best **Place for Performance Workshops**
★ Chapitô, *Costa do Castelo, 1–7 (p 129)*

Best **Fringe Arts Center**
★★ Culturgest, *Rua Arco do Cego (p 129)*

Best **Moviehouse for a Premiere**
★★ Cinema Londres, *Avenida da Liberdade, 174 (p 128)*

Best **Moviehouse for Blockbusters**
★★ Lusomundo, *Amoreiras Shopping (p 128)*

Best **Moviehouse for Obscure Films**
★ Cinemateca, *Rua Barata Salgueiro, 39 (p 128)*

Teatro Nacional de Dona Maria II.

Campo Pequeno Arts & Entertainment

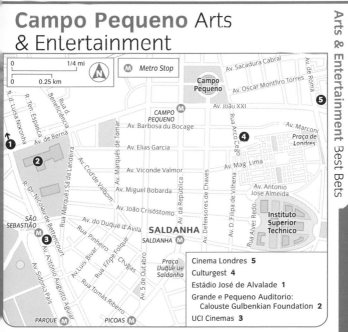

Cinema Londres **5**
Culturgest **4**
Estádio José de Alvalade **1**
Grande e Pequeno Auditorio:
Calouste Gulbenkian Foundation **2**
UCI Cinemas **3**

Belém Arts & Entertainment

Centro Cultural de Belém **2**
Estádio Nacional **1**
Pavilhão Atlântico **3**
Teatro Çamões **4**

City Center Arts & Entertainment

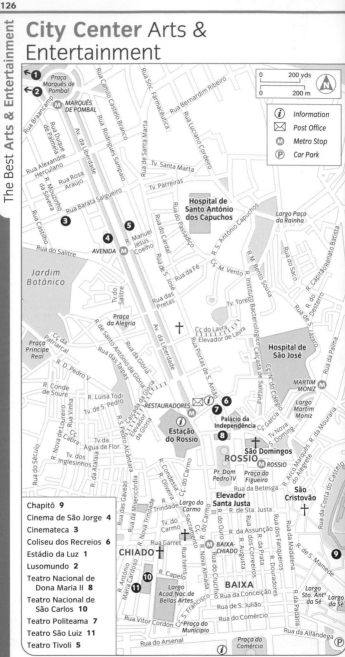

0   200 yds
0   200 m

(i) Information
⊠ Post Office
Ⓜ Metro Stop
Ⓟ Car Park

Chapitô **9**
Cinema de São Jorge **4**
Cinemateca **3**
Coliseu dos Recreios **6**
Estádio da Luz **1**
Lusomundo **2**
Teatro Nacional de
 Dona Maria II **8**
Teatro Nacional de
 São Carlos **10**
Teatro Politeama **7**
Teatro São Luiz **11**
Teatro Tivoli **5**

Arts & Entertainment **A to Z**

Classical Music & Concert Venues

★★ **Centro Cultural de Belém**

BELEM   In the past decade the CCB has become the major cultural center for contemporary arts in Lisbon. Beside concerts and festivals, you can attend classical recitals and performances by a top line-up of jazz and contemporary musicians. In addition, the CCB hosts a full contemporary dance and theater program with some of the most innovative performances from around the world. *Praça do Império.* ☎ *21-361-2400. www.ccb.pt. Tram: 15. Map p 125.*

★★ **Coliseu dos Recreios**

BAIXA   This historic venue dates back to the late 19th century, when it was the concert and show destination. Today it continues to be at the forefront of popular culture, hosting performances by leading musicians, circus acts, and ballet companies, as well as occasional sports events such as kickboxing. *Rua das Portas de Santo Antão.* ☎ *21-324-080. Tickets 20€–180 €. www.coliseulisboa.com. Metro: Rossio, Restauradores. Map p 126.*

★★★ **Grande e Pequeno Auditorio: Calouste Gulbenkian Foundation** SALDANHA   The Gulbenkian Choir and Gulbenkian Orchestra are both respected worldwide for their performances and form part of the Calouste Gulbenkian Foundation, the most prestigious cultural organization in Portugal. They perform an annual season of concerts in the large and small auditorios at the foundation's headquarters alongside a program of visiting international orchestras. *Avenida da Berna.* ☎ *21-782-3030 box office. Tickets 15€–85€. www.musica.gulbenkian. pt. Metro: São Sebastião, Praça de Espanha. Map p 125.*

★★★ **Pavilhão Atlântico**

PARQUE DAS NACOES   Built as part of the Expo '98 project in Parque das Nações, this eye-catching large pavilion looks like a squashed bubble. It hosts major sporting events and concerts by the most renowned national and international stars, as well as congresses and other events. *Rossio dos Olivais.* ☎ *21-891-8409. Tickets 18€–68€. www.pavilhaoatlantico.pt. Metro: Oriente. Map p 125.*

★★★ **Teatro Nacional de São Carlos** BAIRRO ALTO   Built in the Chiado to replace the former opera house destroyed in the 1755 earthquake, this theater boasts a grand neoclassical façade and a sumptuous rococo interior. The annual calendar of events includes opera productions,

The Gulbenkian Orchestra.

Opera fans should check out the productions at Teatro Nacional São Carlos.

concerts by the Orquesta Sinfónica Portuguesa (some of the season takes place at the CCB above), and a few contemporary theater and ballet productions. *Rua de Serpa Pinto, 9.* ☎ *21-325-3045. Tickets 25€–400€. www.saocarlos.pt. Metro: Baixa-Chiado. Map p 126.*

Dance

★★★ **Centro Cultural de Belém** BELEM   See Classical Music & Concert Venues above.

★★ **Teatro Camões** PARQUE DAS NACOES   Home to the Companhia Nacional de Bailado (National Ballet Company) since 2003, and a major performance space with various productions during each season. *Paseo Neptuno.* ☎ *21-325 3045 box office. www.cnb.pt. Metro: Oriente. Map p 125.*

★★★ **Teatro Nacional de São Carlos** BAIRRO ALTO   See Classical Music & Concert Venues above.

Film

★★ **Cinema de São Jorge** AVENIDA   This was the biggest cinema in Portugal when it opened in the 1950s, and was considered state of the art with the latest gadgets such as air-conditioning. Today it has been renovated and hosts premieres, festivals, and other major events. *Avenida da Liberdade, 174.* ☎ *21-310-3400. www.egeac.pt. Tickets various. Metro: Avenida. Map p 126.*

Cinema Londres CAMPO PEQUENO   Now owned by Castello Lopes Cinemas, this compact venue with two screens offers an intimate alternative to the large movie houses in the shopping centers. *Avenida Roma, 7A.* ☎ *21-840-1313. www.castellolopescinemas.com. Tickets 6.30€. Metro: Campo Pequeno, Roma, Areeiro. Map p 125.*

★★ **Cinemateca** AVENIDA   More than just a cinema, this is a museum, archive, exhibition center, and bookshop, all housed in an elegant 19th-century building. It has recently been renovated and hosts two underground movies each month. *Rua Barata Salgueiro, 39.* ☎ *21-359-6262. www.cinemateca.pt. Tickets 2.50€. Metro: Avenida, Rato. Map p 126.*

★★ **Lusomundo** AMOREIRAS/ BENFICA/PARQUE DAS NACOES   These multiplexes in Amoreiras, Colombo, and Vasco da Gama

Advance Tickets & Listings

Turismo de Lisboa publishes a monthly guide called Follow Me Lisboa, which is available at the Lisbon Welcome Center and at many hotels and bars. As well as pages on the latest concerts, theater, festivals, and other events, it has listings and articles on restaurants, bars, attractions, and cultural venues. Also look out for A-Guia's free listing magazine *Lisboa No Bolsa* or browse Sapo's online listings (cultura.sapo.pt). There are several online ticket booking services, including TicketLine (☎ 707-234-234; www.ticketline.pt) and Plateia (☎ 21-434-6304; www.plateia.iol.pt). You can also buy tickets from FNAC (☎ 760-309-330; www.fnac.pt (click on 'Espectáculos')) or buy them in person from any of their stores (see p 82).

shopping centers screen the latest blockbuster releases mostly in the original language with subtitles in Portuguese. www.zonlusomundo. pt. *Amoreiras Shopping, Avenida Engenheiro Duarte Pacheco.* ☎ 21-383-1275. *Metro: Rato. Map p 126.*

Colombo Shopping, Avenida Lusiada. ☎ 21-711-322 *Metro: Colegio Militar.*

Vasco da Gama Shopping, Avenida Dom João II ☎ 21-892-2280. *Metro: Rato.*

UCI Cinemas SALDANHA This cinema in El Corte Inglés department store in Saldanha is the largest in the city with 14 screens, showing the latest releases with Portuguese subtitles. *Avenida Antonio Augusta Aguiar.* ☎ 707-232-221. *www.ucicinemas.pt. Metro: Saldanha. Map p 125.*

Fringe Arts Centers
★ **Chapitô** ALFAMA A cultural center with a restaurant, bar, cafe, theater, and performance arts school, located in the heart of the Alfama. You'll catch *fado*, theater, circus, films and more here, just drop by and see what's on or perhaps even look at joining a workshop. *Costa do Castelo, 1–7.* ☎ 21-885-5550. *www. chapito.org. Tram: 28. Map p 126.*

★★ **Culturgest** CAMPO PEQUENO This multi-arts venue hosts a variety of cutting-edge exhibitions, workshops, theatrical performances, and contemporary dance. *Rua Arco do Cego.* ☎ 21-790-5155. *www. culturgest.pt. Metro: Campo Pequeno. Bus: 54, 56. Map p 125.*

Spectator Sports
★★★ **Estadio da Luz** BENFICA Home to SL Benfica, one of Portugal's premier soccer clubs, it is known to fans as *El Catedral*. If you prepare early enough you can buy tickets online. The ceremony beforehand features a vulture flying from the top of the stadium to a handler on the pitch. A museum here tells

Cinemateca, housed in an elegant 19th-century building.

the club's history, there are tours of the stadium, and a mega-shop full of Benfica kit. *Avenida Lusiada. Tickets from 20€. www.slbenfica.pt. Tour & museum daily 5€–10€. Metro: Colegio Militar. Map p 126.*

★ Estádio José de Alvalade

SANTOS   Home to Lisbon's second soccer team, Sporting Clube de Portugal. You can take a tour of the stadium or visit Mundo Sporting, a museum on the history of the club. *Almeida das Linhas de Torres.* ☎ *707-204-444. Tickets start at 20€. www.sporting.pt. Metro: Campo Grande. Map p 125.*

★ Estádio Nacional OEIRAS   Also

known as Estádio do Jamor, this is Portugal's national soccer ground and hosts the *Taça de Portugal*, the Portuguese Cup. Among Glaswegians it is more renowned though for hosting the 1967 European Cup Final, when Celtic beat Inter Milan 2–1. Whenever Celtic play in Lisbon, fans still make the pilgrimage to relive their team's most glorious moment. *Complex Desportivo do Jamor, Praça da Maratona.* ☎ *21-419-7241. Train Oeiras. Map p 125.*

★★★ Pavilhão Atlântico

PARQUE DAS NACOES   See Classical Music & Concert Venues above.

Theater

★★★ Teatro Nacional de Dona Maria II BAIXA   This theater dom-

inates the north side of Rossio Square with its grand neoclassical façade. Originally built in the 19th century, it suffered a devastating fire in the 1960s and had to be completely reconstructed. It presents a program of both national and international plays, but they are all performed in Portuguese. *Praça Dom Pedro IV.* ☎ *21-325-0835 box office. www.teatro-dmaria.pt. Metro: Rossio, Restauradores. Map p 126.*

Chapitô is located in the heart of the Alfama.

★ Teatro Politeama BAIXA

Located opposite the Coliseu dos Recreios, this grand old theater presents major musicals in Portuguese. *Rua das Portas de Santo Antão, 109.* ☎ *21-324-500. www.teatropoliteama. net. Ticket prices vary. Metro: Restauradores. Map p 126.*

★ Teatro São Luiz CHIADO   Once

the hub of the society set, it has also seen the rise of many Portuguese stars of the stage, and *fado* diva Amália Rodrigues even performed here in 1980. It presents a mixed program of dance, theater, and music. *Rua António Maria Cardoso, 54.* ☎ *21-325-7650. www.teatrosaoluiz. pt. Metro: Baixa-Chiado. Map p 126.*

★ Teatro Tivoli AVENIDA   This

theater started out as a cinema in the 1920s but theatrical productions slowly crept in along with musicals and ballet. Today it is still one of the most striking neoclassical buildings in the Avenida da Liberdade and hosts a mixed program of performances for adults and kids, as well as the occasional film festival. *Avenida da Liberdade, 182.* ☎ *21-357-2025. www. teatro-tivoli.com. Metro: Restauradores, Avenida. Map p 126.* ●

Lodging Best Bets

Best **Historic Hotel**
★★★ Palácio Belmonte $$$$$
Páteo Dom Fradique, 14 (p 144)

Best **Palace Hotel**
★★★ Hotel Lapa Palace $$$$
Rua Pau da Bandeira, 4. (p 141)

Best **Boutique Hotel**
★★★ Bairro Alto Hotel $$$$–$$$$$
c/ de la Marina, 19–21 (p 138)

Best **Modern Hotel**
★★ Hotel Jerónimos 8 $$$ *Rua dos Jerónimos 5 (p 141)*

Best **City Center Location**
Heritage Avenida Liberdade $$$
Avenida da Liberdade, 28. (p 140)

Best **Luxury City Hotel**
★★★ Sofitel $$$–$$$$ *Avenida da Liberdade, 127 (p 145)*

Best **Views**
★★★ Albergaria Senhora do Monte $$ *Calçada do Monte, 39 (p 138)*

Best **Hideaway**
★★★ As Janelas Verdes $$$ *Rua das Janelas Verdes, 47 (p 138)*

Best for **Parks**
★ Residência Avenida Park $$
Avenida Sidónia Pais, 6 (p 144)

Best for **Business**
★★ VIP Executive Barcelona Hotel $$ *Rua Laura Alves, 10 (p 146)*

Best for **Families**
★ Novotel $$ *Avenida José de Malhoa, 1–1A. (p 143)*

Best **Facilities**
★★ Sheraton Lisboa H$$ *Rua Castilho, 1 (p 145)*

Best **Residencial**
★ Residencial Dom Sancho I $
Avenida da Liberdade, 202 (p 144)

Best **on a Budget**
★ Travellers House Hostel $ *Rua Augusta, 89 (p 146)*

Best **Spa Pampering**
★★★ Altis Belém $$$$ *Doca de Bom Sucesso. (p 138)*

Best Boutique Hotel, the Bairro Alto Hotel.

City Center Lodging

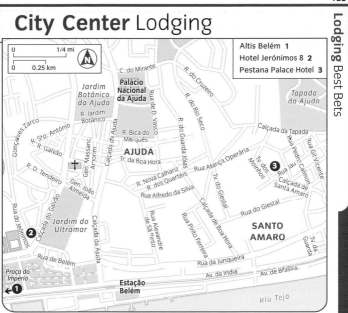

Altis Belém **1**
Hotel Jerónimos 8 **2**
Pestana Palace Hotel **3**

North of Center Lodging

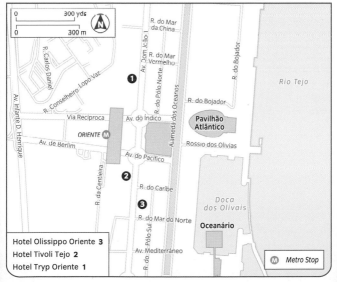

Hotel Olissippo Oriente **3**
Hotel Tivoli Tejo **2**
Hotel Tryp Oriente **1**

Ⓜ Metro Stop

Belém/Alcântara Lodging

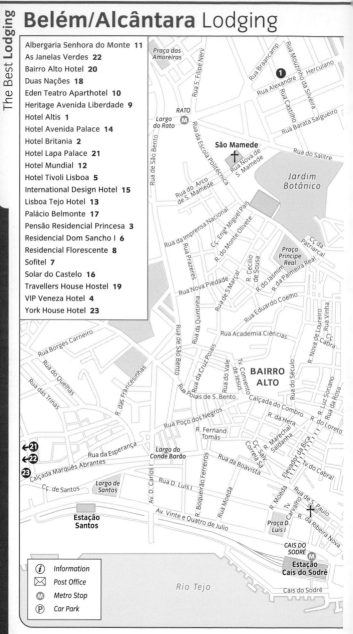

Albergaria Senhora do Monte **11**
As Janelas Verdes **22**
Bairro Alto Hotel **20**
Duas Nações **18**
Eden Teatro Aparthotel **10**
Heritage Avenida Liberdade **9**
Hotel Altis **1**
Hotel Avenida Palace **14**
Hotel Britania **2**
Hotel Lapa Palace **21**
Hotel Mundial **12**
Hotel Tivoli Lisboa **5**
International Design Hotel **15**
Lisboa Tejo Hotel **13**
Palácio Belmonte **17**
Pensão Residencial Princesa **3**
Residencial Dom Sancho I **6**
Residencial Florescente **8**
Sofitel **7**
Solar do Castelo **16**
Travellers House Hostel **19**
VIP Veneza Hotel **4**
York House Hotel **23**

(i) Information
⊠ Post Office
Ⓜ Metro Stop
Ⓟ Car Park

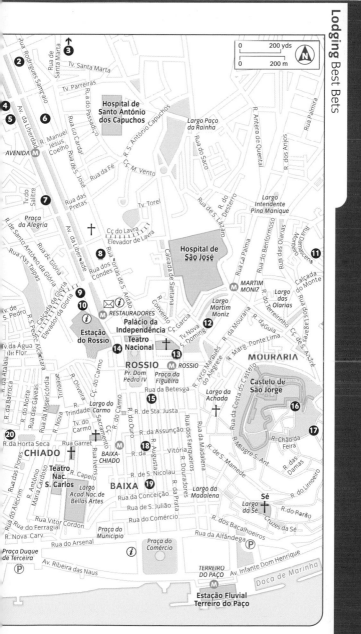

Parque das Nações Lodging

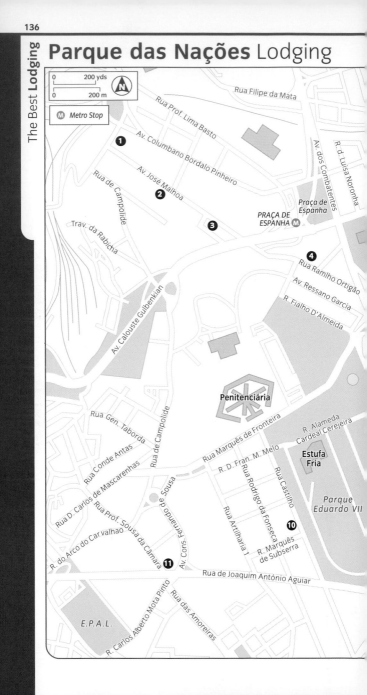

0 | 200 yds
0 | 200 m

Ⓜ Metro Stop

Rua Filipe da Mata

Rua Prof. Lima Basto

❶

Av. Columbano Bordalo Pinheiro

Av. José Malhoa

Rua de Campolide

❷

Trav. da Rabicha

❸

PRAÇA DE ESPANHA

Praça de Espanha

Av. dos Combatentes

R. d. Luísa Noronha

PRAÇA DE ESPANHA Ⓜ

❹

Rua Ramlho Ortigão

Av. Ressano Garcia

R. Fialho D'Almeida

Av. Calouste Gulbenkian

Penitenciária

Rua Gen. Taborda

Rua de Campolide

Rua Conde Antas

Rua D. Carlos de Mascarenhas

Rua Prof. Sousa da Câmara

R. do Arco do Carvalhao

Fernando de Sousa

Av. Cons. Sousa da Câmara

Rua Marquês de Fronteira

R. Alameda Cardeal Cerejeira

R. D. Fran. M. Melo

Rua Rodrigo da Fonseca

Rua Castilho

Estufa Fria

Parque Eduardo VII

Rua Artilharia 1

❿

R. Marquês de Subserra

⓫

Rua de Joaquim António Aguiar

E.P.A.L.

R. Carlos Alberto Mota Pinto

Rua das Amoreiras

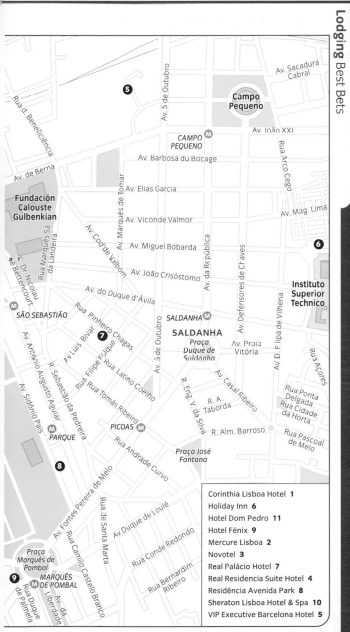

Corinthia Lisboa Hotel **1**
Holiday Inn **6**
Hotel Dom Pedro **11**
Hotel Fénix **9**
Mercure Lisboa **2**
Novotel **3**
Real Palácio Hotel **7**
Real Residencia Suite Hotel **4**
Residência Avenida Park **8**
Sheraton Lisboa Hotel & Spa **10**
VIP Executive Barcelona Hotel **5**

Lisbon **Lodging A to Z**

★★ **Albergaria Senhora do Monte** ALFAMA Located on the slopes of the Alfama, this guesthouse is clean and basic. Some of the rooms have spacious terraces with great views over the Tagus River. *Calçada do Monte, 39.* ☎ *21-886-6002. 28 units. Doubles 70€–120€. AE, MC, V. Tram: 28. Map p 134.*

★★★ **Altis Belém** BELEM With so few hotels in Belém, this new, luxury spa hotel is sure to be a winner. What's more, it's right on the waterfront, many of its discoveries-themed rooms boasting private terraces overlooking the Tagus and the adjacent marina. The indoor pool, hammam, and therapeutic treatments are topped only by the exclusive Feitoria Restaurant, with Michelin-starred chef José Cordeiro at the helm (see p 106). *Doca de Bom Successo.* ☎ *21-040-0200. www.altishotels.com. 55 units. Doubles 370€–640€. AE, DC, MC, V. Tram: 15. Map p 133.*

★★★ **As Janelas Verdes** SANTOS A boutique hotel in a historic 18th-century house next door to the Ancient Art Museum and reputedly where Portuguese writer Eça de Queiros lived in the 19th century. The contemporary furnishings sit well against the backdrop of the building's old architecture. The garden is a quiet shaded retreat and there's a library with a terrace overlooking the river. *Rua das Janelas Verdes, 47.* ☎ *21-396-8143. www. heritage.pt. 29 units. Doubles 138€– 435€. AE, DC, MC, V. Tram: 15, 25. Map p 134.*

★★★ **Bairro Alto Hotel** BAIRRO ALTO In a restored 18th-century building, this boutique hotel deftly combines classic Portuguese décor

Luxury bathroom, Bairro Alto Hotel.

with contemporary touches, including photography by local artists. There's also a restaurant, bar, gym, and wellness center, plus the bonus of Lisbon nightlife on your doorstep. *Praça Luís de Camões, 2.* ☎ *21-340-8288. www.bairroaltohotel.com. 55 units. Doubles 170€–600€. AE, MC, V. Metro: Baixa-Chiado. Tram: 28. Map p 134.*

★★ kids **Corinthia Lisboa Hotel** CAMPOLIDE Close to Lisbon Zoo and with views of the 18th-century aqueduct from the upper floors, this huge hotel has facilities to match. It's regularly used for congresses but it also caters for leisure guests with two restaurants, bar, outdoor pool, and fitness center. *Avenida Columbano Bordalo Pinheiro, 105.* ☎ *21-723-6363. www.corinthiahotels.com. 518 units. Doubles 105€–345€. AE, DC, MC, V. Metro: Praça de Espanha. Map p 136.*

★ **Duas Nações** BAIXA A rarity, this B&B is located right in the heart

Types of Lodging

In Portugal, all accommodations are classified by a starring system within their category, with 5 at the top and 1 at the budget end. Hotels can range from modern towers to boutique hotels. A number of hotels in Lisbon are located in former palaces, usually indicated in the title. *Pousadas* are located in converted historic buildings; the nearest ones to Lisbon are in Queluz and Setúbal. For more information, see www.pousadas.pt (☎ 21-844-2001). Most hotels in Portugal serve breakfast, but do check this at the time of booking. Prices are generally quoted per room rather than per person. There are various kinds of B&B/ boarding houses, called *solar, albergaria, pensão,* and *residencial*. These are often in more traditional buildings with Portuguese tiles. A *pensão* or *residencial* is usually a cheaper option. There are also a number of private hostels in Lisbon with both shared and individual rooms.

of the Baixa. The building is old and the rooms are basic—not all have en suite bathrooms, but most have windows opening onto the vibrant streets outside. Beware, although it's quieter at night, noises echo through these grid-like streets so it's best avoided if you are a light sleeper. *Rua dos Condes de Mon-santo, 2.* ☎ *21-886-6182.* www. duasnacoes.com. *54 units. Doubles*

46€–185€. AE, DC, MC, V. Tram: 15, 28. Metro: Rossio. Map p 134.

★★ Eden Teatro Aparthotel

RESTAURADORES   This stylish Art Deco building was once a theater but was transformed into an aparthotel a few years ago. Right on the Praça dos Restauradores, the studios and apartments face onto an atrium whilst the terrace boasts huge city

The Art Deco Eden Teatro Aparthotel.

Reserving Accommodation

To get the best deals, reserve ahead, particularly if going during the summer months from June to September. June is particularly busy because of Lisbon's festivities. Hotels also fill up around New Year. There are various options for reserving lodging online, including Expedia (www.expedia.com) or the comprehensive Portuguese Maisturismo (www.maisturismo.com). There are some hostels on these websites, otherwise try www.hostels.com or www.lisbonhostels.com.

If arriving in Lisbon without lodging, either ask at the Lisbon Welcome Center (see p 170) or look for a *residencial* or *pensão* in the streets around Rossio Square and off Avenida da Liberdade. If you'd rather stay in a hotel and the city center options are booked out, try the business district, where the hotels can be surprisingly good value and just a metro ride away.

views. *Praça dos Restauradores, 24.* ☎ *21-321-6600. www.viphotels.com. 134 units. Doubles 66€–184€. MC, V. Elevador da Glória. Metro: Restauradores. Map p 134.*

★★★ **Heritage Avenida Liberdade** RESTAURADORES This small boutique hotel deftly combines 18th-century grandeur with understated contemporary style thanks to Portuguese architect Miguel Câncio Martins (whose other projects include the Buddha Bar in Paris and Man Ray in New York). With its sumptuous sofas, low lighting, and a sweet scent, the foyer is as relaxing as the spa and pool downstairs. Rooms feature stylish wallpaper, chaise longues, large, cool en suites, and city center views. *Avenida da Liberdade, 28.* ☎ *21-340-4040. www. heritage.pt. 42 units. Doubles 206€– 253€. AE, DC, MC, V. Metro: Restauradores, Avenida. Map p 134.*

★ **Holiday Inn** SALDANHA Located in the business district, just minutes from the metro station, facilities range from a roof-top pool and mini-gym to a buffet restaurant

and large lobby bar. It's very reasonable but do reserve in advance. *Avenida António José de Almeida, 28-A.* ☎ *21-004-4000. www.ichotelsgroup. com. 169 units. Doubles 60€–150€. AE, DC, MC, V. Metro: Saldanha. Map p 136.*

★★ **Hotel Altis** RATO At this top Lisbon hotel, facilities and comfort beat stylistic statements hands down. Positives include the location, just off the Avenida da Liberdade, the pool and spa treatments, and the superb roof-top views from the restaurant-grill D. Fernando. *Rua Castilho, 11.* ☎ *21-310-6000. www. altishotels.com. 303 units. Doubles 110€–370€. AE, DC, MC, V. Metro: Rato, Avenida. Map p 134.*

★★ **Hotel Avenida Palace** RESTAURADORES Designed by the architect of Rossio Station, this Belle Époque palace-hotel dates back to 1892. Restorations have enhanced the style and décor of the period, with an English-style dark-wood bar, and the Palace Lounge with its 19th-century glass ceiling. *R 1° de Dezembro, 123.* ☎ *21-342-6135.*

www.hotelavenidapalace.pt. 82 units. Doubles 125€–550€. AE, MC, V. Metro: Rossio, Restauradores. Map p 134.

★★ **Hotel Britania** ANJOS Built in the 1940s by famed Portuguese architect Cassiano Branco, this hotel is an Art Deco gem. It has been restored to enhance its original style, while adding a helping of contemporary design. The location on a quiet road off the Avenida da Liberdade means you can escape the city traffic and retreat to the bar and the appealing open fire. *Rua Rodrigues Sampaio, 17.* ☎ *21-315-5016. www.heritage.pt. 30 units. Doubles 215€–340€. AE, DC, MC, V. Metro: Avenida. Map p 134.*

★★★ Hotel Dom Pedro

AMOREIRAS With its blue-mirrored glass exterior, this high-rise hotel reflects the clouds and the Amoreiras shopping center opposite. After a long day of exploring, put your feet up in the traditional comfort of your room, catch up on e-mail, or enjoy dinner in the Italian restaurant. Guests in the more expensive rooms are given access to the VIP lounge with complimentary drinks and far-reaching city views. *Avenida Eng. Duarte Pacheco 24.* ☎ *21-330-0541. www.dompedro.com. 263*

units. Doubles 130€–2647€. AE, MC, V. Metro: Rato. Map p 136.

★★ **Hotel Fénix** PARQUE You can't miss this hotel on the edge of Praça Marquês de Pombal with its name in lights emblazoned across the top. At the heart of Lisbon's road network, business, leisure, and culture activities are within easy reach and catered for in the hotel. You can hang out in the vast indoor lounges or the palm-filled atrium garden. *Praça Marquês de Pombal, 8.* ☎ *21-386-2121. www.hoteisfenix.com. 192 units. Doubles 70€–202€. AE, DC, MC, V. Metro: Marquês de Pombal. Map p 136.*

★★ **Hotel Jerónimos 8** BELEM Opened in 2007 and offering a rare opportunity to stay in Belém, this contemporary hotel has quickly become part of the exclusive Design Hotels club. There's a retro-trendy bar on the ground floor and some of the contemporary rooms lead onto a decked terrace where you can relax in the evening. *Rua dos Jerónimos.* ☎ *21-360-0900. www.almeida hotels.com. 65 units. Doubles 90€–270€. AE, DC, MC, V. Tram: 15. Map p 133.*

★★★ Hotel Lapa Palace

LAPA A city oasis where you can

The pool and gardens at Hotel Lapa Palace.

indulge in luxurious spa treatments, lie out by the pool in the lush gardens, join the ladies of Lisbon for afternoon tea, and enjoy intimate dining in Restaurante Lapa. Choose from rooms in the palace, garden or villa wings, or splash out on the tower room with outdoor terrace and 360 degree views. *Rua Pau da Bandeira, 4.* ☎ *21-330-0541. www.lapapalace.com. 109 units. Doubles 275€–725€. AE, MC, V. Tram: 15. Map p 134.*

★★ **Hotel Mundial** MARTIM MONIZ   Just a few minutes from Rossio Square, this large hotel has comfortable rooms and substantial breakfasts. It prides itself on its eating and drinking facilities, which include wine-tasting sessions in the bar and the Varanda de Lisboa restaurant with panoramic views. *Praça Martim Moniz.* ☎ *21-884-2000. www.hotel-mundial.pt. 350 units. Doubles 92€–300€. AE, DC, MC, V. Metro: Martim Moniz. Tram: 12, 28. Map p 134.*

★★ **Hotel Olissippo Oriente** PARQUE DAS NACOES   The modern brightness of the exterior is reflected inside with crisp white bed linen, floral wallpaper, and plump cushions. There's a similar feel throughout the hotel's bars and public areas, and it is close to Lisbon's FIL conference center. *Avenida Dom João II.* ☎ *21-892-9100. www.olissippohotels.com. 182 units. Doubles 110€–250€. AE, DC, MC, V. Metro: Oriente. Map p 133.*

★★★ **Hotel Tivoli Lisboa** AVENIDA   If you want luxury and comfort in the city center, this is a popular choice for both executives and tourists on short breaks. The décor is traditional, the restaurants are smart, one with a roof terrace, plus there's a piano bar and an outdoor pool in a leafy garden. *Avenida da Liberdade, 185.* ☎ *21-319-8900.*

www.tivolihotels.com. 329 units. Doubles 149€–347€. AE, DC, MC, V. Metro: Avenida, Restauradores. Map p 134.

★★ **Hotel Tivoli Tejo** PARQUE DAS NACOES   Suitable for both business trips and family stays, this contemporary hotel in the heart of Parque das Nações is clean and relaxed. The pool and health club will keep both kids and adults happy, along with its ample buffet breakfast, restaurants, parking, and Wi-Fi. For quieter rooms, request accommodation on the upper floors. *Avenida Dom João II.* ☎ *21-891-5100. www.tivolihotels.com. 279 units. Doubles 135€–274€. AE, MC, V. Metro: Oriente. Map p 133.*

★★ **Hotel Tryp Oriente** PARQUE DAS NACOES   One of just a handful of places to stay in this part of town, this is a high-rise, modern hotel with views across the park. Alongside a restaurant and bar, the hotel offers Wi-Fi and easy access to transport, shopping, and the airport. *Avenida*

Hotel Mundial has great views of the city.

Hotel Olissippo Oriente.

Dom João II. ☎ *21-893-000. www. solmelia.com. 207 units. Doubles 72€–155€. AE, DC, MC, V. Metro: Oriente. Map p 133.*

★★ International Design

Hotel ROSSIO   This celebrated new design hotel has an enviable position overlooking Rossio Square. The ultra-modern guest rooms range from cool and neutral to bold and bright décor and furnishings, based around concepts of pop, zen, tribu, and urban. The restaurant and bar are equally as fashionable, with retro sofas and a trendy terrace. *Rua das Betesga, 3.* ☎ *21-324-0990. internacional.lisbonhotels.it. 55 units. Doubles 98€–200€. AE, MC, V. Metro: Rossio. Map p 134.*

★ Lisboa Tejo Hotel BAIXA

The hotel reception greets guests with a funky mix of bare brick and contemporary wood and glass. Rooms are pretty basic but perfectly comfortable and the decent breakfast of cereals, fresh fruit, and hot eggs available here should keep you going through to lunch. *Rua dos Condes de Monsanto, 2.*

☎ *21-886-6182. www.evidencia hoteis.com. 58 units. Doubles 80€– 164€. AE, DC, MC, V. Metro: Rossio. Tram: 15, 28. Map p 134.*

★★ kids Mercure Lisboa CAM-

POLIDE   This hotel might not be downtown, but it's just a 10-minute walk from Lisbon Zoo and the Parque Florestal de Monsanto, and the nearest metro is only minutes away. There's a pool, open year round, a restaurant and a bar. *Avenida José Malhoa, 23.* ☎ *21-720-8000. www.mercure.com. 104 units. Doubles 61€–120€. AE, DC, MC, V. Metro: Campolilde. Map p 136.*

★ kids Novotel CAMPOLIDE

Large, modern, and comfortable, this renowned hotel is located conveniently between Lisbon Zoo and the Gulbenkian Museum. It's ideal for families as there's an outdoor pool (you can order food there too), and play areas for kids both inside and outside the hotel. *Avenida José de Malhoa, 1–1A.* ☎ *21-330-0541. www.novotel.com. 249 units. Doubles 68€–90€. AE, DC, MC, V.*

Metro: Praça de Espanha. Map p 136.

★★★ Palácio Belmonte

ALFAMA A romantic hideaway just outside the walls of the Castelo de São Jorge, this 15th-century palace-hotel has 10 unique suites, individually dressed with Portuguese tiles, antiques, and art, and named after historic Portuguese personalities from writers and travelers to Jesuits and philosophers. The library has around 4,000 tomes, or you can take a dip in the black marble pool. *Páteo Dom Fradique, 14.* ☎ *21-881-6609. www.palaciobelmonte.com. 10 units. Suites 400€–1200€. AE, DC, MC, V. Tram: 28. Map p 134.*

★ Pensão Residencial Princesa

ARROIOS To the east of the Avenida da Liberdade, this straightforward, comfy B&B-style accommodation is real value for money. Located off the main thoroughfare, this is also a quieter choice. *Rua Gomes Freire, 130.* ☎ *21-319-3070. www.residencial-princesa.pt. 47 units. Doubles 45€–75€. AE, DC, MC, V. Metro: Avenida. Map p 134.*

★★★ Pestana Palace Hotel

ALCANTARA This sets a tone of luxury from the moment the uniformed doorman opens the car door to the grand high-ceilinged accommodation complete with gilt-edged cornices. It has marble floors, sweeping stairs, chandeliers, antiques, painted ceilings, lush tropical gardens, and two pools. There are also two restaurants and a bar with views across the grounds. *Rua Jau, 54.* ☎ *21-361-5600. www. pestana.com. 190 units. Doubles 161€–305€. AE, DC, MC, V. Tram: 15. Map p 133.*

★★ kids Real Palácio Hotel

PARQUE A 17th-century former palace and an adjacent building have been combined to create this quality hotel. Large and pink on the outside, the interior is quite traditional and functional, and there is a gym and sauna. Useful facilities for families include kids' furniture, toys, and menus, and a babysitting service. *Rua Tomás Ribeiro, 115.* ☎ *21-319-9500. www.hoteisreal.com. 147 units. Doubles 125€–260€. AE, MC, V. Metro: Parque. Map p 136.*

★★★ Real Residencia Suite Hotel

PARQUE Cheaper than sister venue, Real Palacio Hotel, this aparthotel has 1- and 2-bed suites, with facilities for families (kids' furniture, menus, and babysitting), plus you can still use the gym facilities at the Real Palacio. The apartments have equipped kitchenettes for self-catering and there's a restaurant/cafe/bar. *Rua Ramalho Ortigão, 41.* ☎ *21-382-2900. www.hoteisreal. com. 24 units. Doubles 85€–225€. AE, MC, V. Metro: São Sebastião. Map p 136.*

★ Residência Avenida Park

SAO SEBASTIAO If you're lucky you might get one of the rooms with a view over Parque Eduardo VII. Portuguese touches such as traditional tiles in the bathroom blend well with modern and bright public spaces downstairs. *Avenida Sidónia Pais, 6.* ☎ *21-353-2181. www.avenidapark.com. 40 units. Doubles 70€–140€. AE, DC, MC, V. Metro: Marquês de Pombal. Map p 134.*

★ Residencial Dom Sancho I

AVENIDA In an 18th-century building on the Avenida da Liberdade, this B&B has a local flavor with white-washed walls, Portuguese antique-style furnishings, and decorative tiled panels on the walls. *Avenida da Liberdade, 202.* ☎ *21-354-8042. www.domsancho.com. 40 units. Doubles 54€–100€. AE, MC, V. Metro: Avenida, Restauradores. Map p 134.*

★ Residencial Florescente

BAIXA This bright and typically

Real Residência Suite.

Portuguese B&B is located on a lively street buzzing with restaurants. Rooms are basic and, as this is a busy street for socializing, noise can be an issue, but for such a central location it's not expensive. *Rua das Portas de Santo Antão, 99.* ☎ *21-342-6609. www.residencial florescente.com. 68 units. Doubles 55€–65€. AE, DC, MC, V. Metro: Rossio, Restauradores. Map p 134.*

★★★ **Sheraton Lisboa Hotel & Spa** PARQUE   The standard rooms at this landmark hotel have been brought up to date with warm brown hues and deluxe rooms with glass-walled en suites. Located close to Parque Eduardo VII, the hotel is perfect for both business and leisure stays, boasting several meeting rooms as well as a gourmet restaurant and top-floor cocktail bar. There's also a spa, gym, and outdoor pool. *Rua Castilho, 1.* ☎ *21-312-0000. www.starwoodhotels.com. 369 units. Doubles 143€–240€. AE, MC, V. Metro: Pombal. Map p 136.*

★★★ **Sofitel** AVENIDA   This is a luxury hotel in the heart of the tree-lined Avenida da Liberdade. You can expect an understated mix of traditional and modern décor in the guestrooms and adventurous but elegant dining in its Ad-Lib restaurant (see p 108). *Avenida da Liberdade, 127.* ☎ *21-322 8300. www.sofitel.com. 171 units. Doubles 89€ 158€. AE, MC, V. Metro: Avenida. Map p 134.*

★★★ **Solar do Castelo** ALFAMA   Within the grounds of the Castelo de São Jorge, this is believed to be on the site of the castle kitchens; there's still a medieval cistern here (but don't worry, it's not for guest use). Most of the building dates to around the 18th century, but the thick stone walls really give it the feel of a castle, while the patio and pond at the back seem more colonial. The interiors have been carefully restored with a mix of antique style and contemporary furnishings. *Rua das Cozinhas, 2.* ☎ *21-880-6050. www.heritage.pt. 14 units. Doubles 270€–660€. AE, DC, MC, V. Tram: 28. Map p 134.*

★★ **Travellers House Hostel**
BAIXA When it comes to hostels, this is a popular choice, so book well ahead. Located in the heart of the Baixa, the décor is homely and on-trend, with large corner sofas, bean-bags, papered feature walls, and glitzy light shades. Residents can cook dinner, relax in front of the wide-screen TV, watch DVDs, borrow a book, or use the Internet. Dorms sleep four to six people but there are double rooms for couples. *1st floor, Rua Augusta, 89.* ☎ *21-346-1058. www.lisbonpoetshotel.com. Shared rooms, per person 20€; double room per person 35€. Map p 134.*

★★ **VIP Executive Barcelona Hotel** ALVALADE In the heart of Lisbon's financial district (and not far from the Calouste Gulbenkian Foundation), this hotel is up to date and smart, and has a bar with invit-ing armchairs for a relaxing drink. *Rua Laura Alves, 10.* ☎ *21-795-4273. www.viphotels.com. 125 units. Doubles 43€–80€. MC, V. Metro: Campo Pequeno. Tram: 15, 28. Map p 136.*

★ **VIP Veneza Hotel** AVENIDA
Handily central, this occupies a con-verted 19th-century building where you can expect classical-style com-fort but not luxury for your money. However, it has retained some of its historic grandeur such as the wood-paneled sitting room and a few stained-glass windows. *Avenida da Liberdade, 189.* ☎ *21-352-2618. www.viphotels.com. 37 units. Dou-bles 85€–101€. MC, V. Metro: Ave-nida, Restauradores. Map p 134.*

★★★ **York House Hotel** SAN-TOS A boutique hotel in a 17th-century former Carmelite convent, the décor mixes classical and mod-ern chic with contemporary furnish-ings. Add the award-winning, intimate restaurant and leafy ter-race, and this makes an ideal hide-away for a romantic weekend. *Rua das Janelas Verdes, 32.* ☎ *21-396-2435. www.yorkhouselisboa.com. 32 units. Doubles 110€–260€. AE, DC, MC, V. Tram: 15, 25. Map p 134.* ●

VIP Executive Barcelona Hotel.

Costa do Estoril Beach Hopping

1. Carcavelos
2. Estoril
3. Cascais
4. Guincho

Colares

N247

Sintra

N249

N247

Azoia

Parque Natural Sintra Cascais

ATLANTIC OCEAN

4

Alcabideche

N9

A5

N9-1

Estoril

2

3

Cascais

1

| 0 | 2 mi |
| 0 | 2 km |

O ne reason I find Lisbon so manageable even in the heat of summer is that it's so easy to escape for a swim in the ocean. Just a short trip out of Lisbon, the Costa do Estoril has beaches all the way along the coast, ideal for both families and surfers. Some of these locations are reachable by train (Cais do Sodré station in Lisbon), but for others you'll need a car.

Estoril Beach.

Guincho Kite Surfing.

1 ★★ **Carcavelos.** From Carcavelos station, it's about a seven-minute walk to the beach. Long and sandy, and overlooked by the large Forteza de São Julião da Barra (St Julian of Barra Fortress), it's popular with surfers although during the summer you will need an early start to avoid the daytrippers. Windsurf Café on Avenida Marginal (☎ 21-457-8965. www.windsurfcafe.pt) runs courses. *By train: Carcavelos station. By car: N6 coast road or A5 motorway, jct. 8.*

2 ★★ **Estoril.** Between Cascais and Estoril, sandy Praia de Tamariz is dotted with sunshades and is popular with surfers. The original 19th-century resort is nearby, consisting of hotels, grandiose mansions, and the Estoril Casino. Between here and Carcavelos, several smaller beaches—São Pedro, São João, and Parede—attract families and surfers. *By train: Parede, São Pedro, São João, Estoril stations. By car: N6 coast road or A5 motorway, jct. 8.*

3 ★★ **Cascais.** Cascais has various beaches, plus the added bonus of attractions such as the marina and the Municipal Museum. The fishermen bring their daily catch into Praia dos Pescadores, so head instead to the tiny, sheltered Praia de Rainha, where kids can paddle, or Praia da Conceição and Praia da Duquesa for decent food and drink facilities. *See p 150.*

4 **Guincho.** Exposed to the Atlantic wind and waves, this hosts major surfing competitions. A cycle path runs from Cascais, passing the Boca do Inferno (see p 152) en route, and if you have a car, follow the coast road to the dramatic cliffs and lighthouse at Cabo da Roca, the most westerly point in mainland Europe. *By car: A5 from Lisbon, then follow signs to Guincho Beach. Estrada do Guincho from Cascais.*

Fishing boats moored opposite a beach in Cascais.

Cascais & Estoril

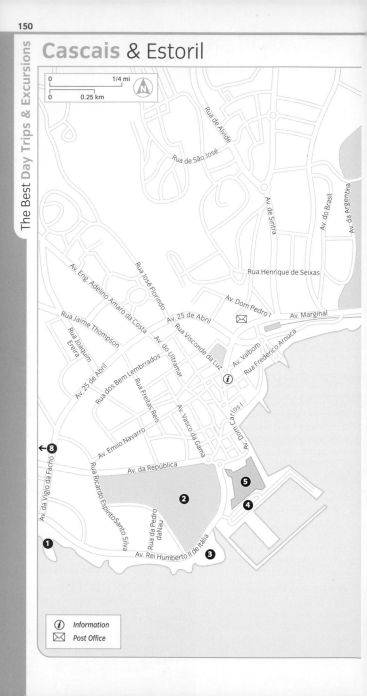

(i) Information

✉ Post Office

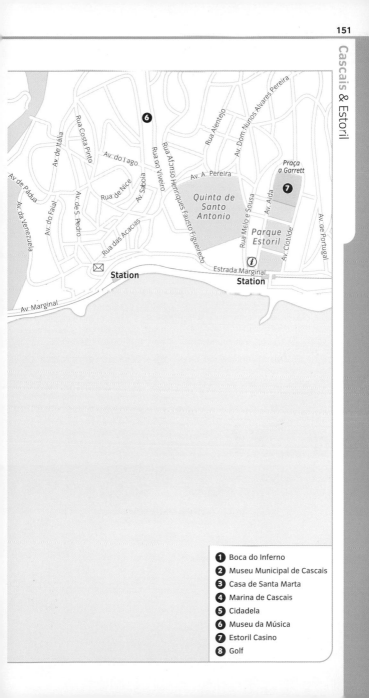

1 Boca do Inferno
2 Museu Municipal de Cascais
3 Casa de Santa Marta
4 Marina de Cascais
5 Cidadela
6 Museu da Música
7 Estoril Casino
8 Golf

Cascais and Estoril have been popular with Lisboetas since the train line opened in the late 19th century and despite development in recent decades, you can still see the fanciful mansions built by the rich former residents, some of which are now museums. Today the whole Estoril coast is one big summer playground focusing on the resorts of Estoril and Cascais.

① ★★ Boca do Inferno. It takes about 15 minutes to walk here from Cascais Marina, past the lighthouse then to a small market selling a mixture of old tat and souvenir ceramics. The 'Mouth of Hell', as it's known in English, is an ancient rock cavern, whipped away by the sea over millions of years. Look out for the plaque regarding occultist Aleister Crowley (1875–1947). He reputedly faked a suicide note, but in reality had skipped off to Spain to read reports about his own death. Today there are steps and railings so you can peer over the edge in relative safety. ⏱ *1 hr. Estrada do Guincho.*

② ★ Museu Municipal de Cascais. Cascais's Municipal Museum is housed in a striking gray brick and cream mock-Gothic mansion, complete with misshaped windows and a tower. Close to the sea, it has a high-tide private pool and beach.

Inside the palace discover courtyards with Moorish-style fountains, elaborate arches, and large rooms with over-the-top gilt-edged mirrors, Indo-Portuguese furniture and a library of books dating back to the 17th century. Outside, find the chapel—Capela de São Sebastião—decorated with blue and white tiles, and a peaceful park where you can wander among the peacocks in the mini-zoo or stop for a coffee at the cafe in the center. ⏱ *1½–2hrs. Palácio dos Condes de Castro Guimarães, Avenida Rei Humberto II de Itália.* ☎ *21-482-5401. Free admission. Tues–Sun 10am–5pm.*

③ ★ Casa de Santa Marta. On the road between the marina and Boca do Inferno, this striking colonial-style pastel-orange mansion perches on a rocky promontory overlooking the sea. At the end is the eye-catching blue-and-white

Serene tiled chapel & gardens at the Museu Municipal de Cascais.

The 19th-century lighthouse and museum.

19th-century lighthouse, built on a recently renovated 17th-century fort, and housing an exhibition of lighthouse history and memorabilia. 🕐 *30–60 min. Rua do Farol.* ☎ *21-481-5328 Admission 5€. May–Sept Tues–Sun 10am–6pm.*

④ ★ Marina de Cascais. This attractive marina can get busy, with various competitions throughout the year and opportunities for sailing and fishing trips (Clube Naval de Cascais ☎ 21-483-0125). Explore the area further and you'll discover a whole row of restaurants and bars hidden from view. 🕐 *30–60 min. Marina reception* ☎ *21 482-4899. www.marina-cascais.com. Office summer 9am–7pm; winter 9am–6pm.*

Practical Matters: Cascais & Estoril

From Lisbon take the Avenida da Brasília past Belém and out along the N6 coast road or the A5 motorway and exit for Cascais or Estoril. Trains leave frequently (30 minutes; www.cp.pt) from Lisbon's Cais do Sodré station and take approximately 40 minutes to Cascais. The **Tourist Information Office** (☎ 21-486-8204; www.estorilcoast-tourism.com) is at Rua Visconde da Luz, 14. The tourist office offers a free bicycle lending service; just take along your passport to the booths opposite the train station and by the Cidadela (Open daily 9am–6pm).

    Farol Design Hotel, (☎ 21-482-3490; www.farol.com; doubles 110€–250€), is a contemporary boutique hotel with ocean views, funky design throughout, and a pool; **Hotel Cascais Miragem** (☎ 21-006-0600; www.cascaismirage.com) is worth the extra expense for its indulgent breakfasts, on-site gym and spa, and spacious rooms, many with spectacular sea views.

Boca do Inferno also known as the 'Mouth of Hell'.

⑤ ★★ Cidadela. Although this large fortress dominates the promontory at Cascais, all you can do at present is walk around the looming walls, although there are plans to develop it into a museum. If your Portuguese is good enough, read the note on how the current plans are going. ⌚ *5–10 min.*

⑥ ★ Museu da Musica. This small but unusual collection of Portuguese musical instruments was

Go sailing from the Marina de Cascais.

collected by a Corsican ethnomusicologist, Michel Giacometti (1929–90) during the 20th century and acquired from him by Mantero Belard, a local patron of the arts. The museum also houses the assets of Portuguese composer Fernando Lopes-Graça (1906–94). The house itself was designed by renowned Portuguese architect Raul Lino (1879–1974), also responsible for designing various other properties in Estoril and Cascais, including the Casa de Santa Maria (see above). He created a mansion house that displays Moorish influences in its arched windows and castellated tower. Tours of the whole house are by prior arrangement only. ⌚ *1 hr. Avenida de Saboia, 1146, Monte Estoril* ☎ *21-481-5901. Tues–Sun 10am–1pm & 2–5pm.*

⑦ Estoril Casino. For many this venue is the highlight of their trip to Estoril. Apart from being the largest casino in Europe, you can enjoy a good dinner here, followed by a glamorous show. Upstairs there are several jewelers and an art gallery, and

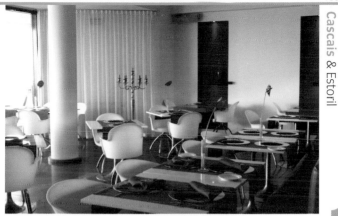

Farol Design Hotel.

the gardens outside are an elaborate light show, with bulbs strung from tree to tree. Men should wear a jacket and tie and women evening dress. *Praça José Teodoro dos Santos* ☎ 21-466-7700. Daily 3pm–3am.

8 ★ Golf. There isn't enough space here for a comprehensive guide to the golf courses on the

Costa do Estoril, as there are seven 18-hole courses and one 9 hole course. Two of the best include: **Quinta da Marinha Oitavos Golf,** just west of Cascais and set in 110 hectares of pine woods, where you can play against a backdrop of the Atlantic Ocean and the Sintra Mountains; and **Penha Longa Atlantic,** at the foot of the Sintra hills.

Estoril Casino.

Sintra

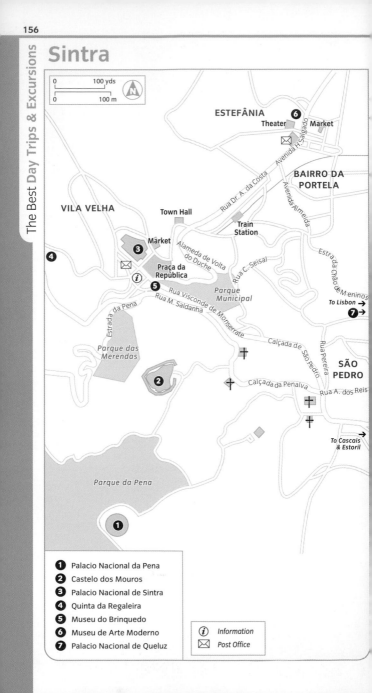

| 0 | 100 yds |
| 0 | 100 m |

ESTEFÂNIA ❻
Theater   Market
✉

BAIRRO DA
PORTELA

Avenida H. Salgado

Rua Dr. A. da Costa

Avenida Almeida

VILA VELHA   Town Hall

❸   Market
✉   Train
Station

Alameda de Volta
do Duche

Estrada da Chão de Meninos

❹

ⓘ   Praça da
República

❺   Rua Visconde de Monserrate   Rua C. Seisal

Rua M. Saldanha   Parque
Municipal   To Lisbon →
❼ →

Estrada da Pena

Parque das
Merendas   Calçada de São Pedro   Rua Pereira

❷   ✝   SÃO
PEDRO

✝   Calçada da Penalva   Rua A. dos Reis

✝

Parque da Pena   ◆   To Cascais
& Estoril →

✝

❶

❶ Palacio Nacional da Pena
❷ Castelo dos Mouros
❸ Palacio Nacional de Sintra
❹ Quinta da Regaleira
❺ Museu do Brinquedo
❻ Museu de Arte Moderno
❼ Palacio Nacional de Queluz

ⓘ Information
✉ Post Office

Just a short train ride from Lisbon is the UNESCO World Heritage Site of Sintra, a favorite summer retreat of the Portuguese royal family for centuries. Take your time to soak up Sintra's playful curiosities, the spectacularly lavish 19th-century mansions, and the delicious taste of queijadas, a local specialty cheese cake.

❶ ★★★ Palacio Nacional da Pena.

Built on a hilltop, on the site of a 15th-century convent by Dom Fernando de Saxe-Coburg (king consort to Dona Maria II from 1836–53) as a summer palace in the 19th century, this is an extraordinary over-the-top romantic fantasy. It's pure pastiche: candy-colored yellow and pink, with neo-Gothic turrets and castellations, Moorish-style horseshoe arches, walls covered in tiles, neo-Manueline motifs, mythological characters around windows, and even an arch with the same diamond-shaped bricks as the Casa dos Bicos in Lisbon (p 24). It holds a commanding position looking across the Sintra hills, with the outskirts of Lisbon in view, and it fits perfectly into the Pena Park's lush green grounds, brimming with monuments and grottos. Only the chapel remained standing after the 1755 earthquake. Now incorporated into the palace, its retable has been restored to reveal the illustrious detail of Nicolas de Chaterenne's carved designs. 🕐 1½–2hrs. ☎ 21-910-5340. www.parquesdesintra.pt Admission 12€ Apr-Sep; 8€ rest of year; 9€ 6-17s and seniors; 9€ youth card holder; free under 6s; 32€ family; 1€ discount to all during happy hour (daily 9.30am-11am); further discounts for visits to park only, park & chapel only. Open Apr-Sep daily 9.45am-7pm (last tickets 6.15pm); Oct-Mar daily 10am-6pm (last tickets 5pm).

❷ ★ Castelo dos Mouros.

From the Pena Palace you can walk downhill to the Moorish Castle, which dates to around the 9th century, when the Moors (the Muslims of north African origin) built a settlement here. Occupied alternately by the Moors and Christians, it was finally handed over voluntarily to the Portuguese after D Afonso Henrique's taking of Lisbon in 1147.

Palacio Nacional da Pena.

Over time it lost its strategic importance, falling into decline from around the 14th century. There isn't a great deal left, but the battlements are impressive. If your legs can take it, climb the steps to the top of the battlements for unbeatable views up to the Pena Palace, of Sintra and the National Palace below, and across the Sintra hills all the way to the Atlantic Ocean. You can catch the circular bus back into town (see below) but rather than returning to the entrance, follow the path through the woods that winds down into town. 🕐 *1–1½ hrs. Parques de Sintra, Monte de Lua.* ☎ *21-910-7970. www.parques desintra.pt. Admission 6€; 5€ 6–17 years and seniors; free under 6s. May–Sept daily 9:30am–8pm; Oct–Apr daily 10am–5pm.*

Palacio Nacional de Sintra.

❸ ★ Palacio Nacional de Sintra. The first feature you will notice about this palace at the heart of Sintra's town center is the eye-catching, outsized chimneys, which you can view from the castle's turrets. In contrast to Pena Palace, this building evolved gradually over time, mostly during the 15th and 16th centuries. Although it was built on the site of a former Arab residence, the 15th-century Moorish-style tiles in the central patio and Arab room are something of a nod to the residence that stood here previously. The blue-and-green geometrical designs show the early developments of Portugal's tile culture. Other areas worth lingering are the Swan Room for Manueline motifs, and in the Coat of Arms chamber look up to view the painted motifs of Dom Manuel and 72 noble Portuguese families. 🕐 *1½–2hrs. Largo Rainha Dona Amélia.* ☎ *21-910-6840. Admission 7€; free Sundays and bank holidays until 2pm for under 14s; 50% discount for seniors.*

Practical Matters: Sintra

By car from Lisbon, take the IC-19 in the direction of Sintra and then either the N9, exiting at the next junction for Sintra, or from the IC-19 take the more scenic N249 into the town. Trains leave frequently (every 15 minutes) from Lisbon's Rossio station, taking approximately 25 minutes to Queluz and 40 minutes to Sintra (if you want to go to the coastal resort of Maça on the tram, alight at Portela de Sintra; otherwise continue to the end of the line). The main **Posto de Turismo** is on the Praça da República, 23 (☎ 21-923-1157). A frequent bus (no 434, 4.35€) connects the station, town centre, Castelo dos Mouros and Palacio Nacional da Pena, though I much prefer walking up the path to see the views unfold (the tourist office here can mark you up a map showing the route up).

Eating & Staying in Sintra

Lodging: Hotel Tivoli Palácio de Seteais is a luxury former palace just past the Regaleira Gardens on the outskirts of Sintra. (Rua Barbosa de Bocage; ☎ 21-923-3200; www.tivolihotels.com; doubles 200€–280€; AE, DC, MC, V). **Hotel Tivoli Sintra** (Praça da República; ☎ 21-923-7200; www.tivolihotels.com; doubles 75€–105€) is a lackluster block of a hotel with a dated interior but it's comfortable enough and located right in the heart of the town. **Penha Longa Golf & Hotel Resort** (Estrada da Lagoa Azul; ☎ 21-924-9011; www. penhalonga.com; doubles 175€–2100€) is a large golf resort in the Sintra hills.

Dining: Cozinha Velha (menu 22€–30€) is a renowned traditional restaurant in the former kitchens of the Palácio Nacional de Queluz (Largo do Palácio Nacional de Queluz; ☎ 21-435-6158). **Pateo do Garrett** (9.50€–22€) is an elegant restaurant in the heart of the town with Portuguese and international cuisine (Praça da República, 32; ☎ 21-923-2375).

Thurs–Tues 9:30am–5:30pm (last admission 5pm).

❹ ★ Quinta da Regaleira. Walk out of the town center (or take the bus) to reach the Regaleira Gardens— it's worth the effort. The estate had various owners before it was developed into the current landscape and was constructed between 1904 and 1911 by designer Luigi Manini (1848–1936), on the orders of the owner António August Carvalho Monteiro (1848–1920). Explore the labyrinth of pathways leading past mythological characters, niches, and watery grottoes, a chapel filled with erroneously mixed symbols of masonry and the Order of Christ, and a small neoclassical house. The idea was to create a mixture of universal and Portuguese mythical traditions, so you'll have to work hard to separate fact and fantasy. ⏲ *1–1½hrs Rua Barbosa de Bocage.* ☎ *21-910-6650. Admission 6€; youth card holders 4€; seniors 3€; free under 9s; family 18€. Apr–Sept daily 10:30am–7:30pm; Oct, Feb & Mar*

Quinta da Regaleira.

The 18th-century Palacio Nacional de Queluz.

daily 10am–6:30pm; Nov–Jan daily 10am–5:30pm (last admission 30 mins before closing).

⑤ Museu do Brinquedo. Sintra's Toy Museum is a treasure trove of playthings from the past. You'll take a trip back to your youth and beyond with everything on display from old tin cars and porcelain dolls to clockwork trains and Dinky toys. 🕐 *1hr. Rua Visconde de Monserrate, 28* ☎ *21-924-2171. www. museu-do-brinquedo.pt. Admission 4€; 2€ 3–16s, youth card holders, seniors. Tues–Sun 10am–6pm.*

⑥ ★ Museu de Arte Moderno. This palatial building hosts temporary exhibitions by internationally renowned artists focusing on movements such as Surrealism, Abstraction, Minimalism, Pop Art, and Photography in the 90s. The Berardo Foundation has an outstanding Art Deco collection on

display here. 🕐 *1–1½ hrs. Avenida Heliodoro Salgado* ☎ *21-924-8170. Admission 3€. Open Tues–Sun 10am–6pm.*

⑦ ★ Palacio Nacional de Queluz. This 18th-century pink palace, located between Lisbon and Sintra, has rooms of period furniture, detailed cornices, and heavy chandeliers, but for me the formal gardens outside are the main delight, with neatly trimmed hedges and elaborate baroque fountains. The restaurant in the former royal kitchens is one of the best for Portuguese dining in the Lisbon area and known as the Cozinha Velha. 🕐 *1½–2hrs. Largo do Palácio de Queluz,* ☎ *21-434-3860. Admission: 7€; 60% youth card; 50% seniors; free under 15 years and Sun until 2pm. May–Sept daily 10am–6pm; Oct–Apr daily 10am–5pm.* ●

The
Savvy Traveler

Before You Go

ICEP Portugal—Portuguese Trade and Tourism Office

In the US: 590 Fifth Ave., New York, NY 10036 (☎ 646-723-0200); 185 Berry Street, Suite 5511, San Francisco, CA 94107 (☎ 415-391-7080). **In Canada:** 60 Bloor St. W., Suite 400, Toronto, Ontario M4W 3B8 (☎ 416-921-4925). **In the UK:** 11 Belgrave Sq., London SW1X 8PP (☎ 0845-355-1212).

The Best Time to Go

The Portuguese have their summer vacation from June till September and many *Lisboetas* leave the city at this time. It's not necessarily the heat they're escaping, as Lisbon's position at the mouth of the River Tagus means it's relieved by an Atlantic breeze. However, many take their summer break after Lisbon's festivities, which spread throughout June but dominate the first two weeks. The festivities also attract visitors in their hordes, so make sure you reserve your hotel well ahead if coming at this time. Afterwards, the locals are ready for a rest but the city continues to fill with tourists, mostly Europeans who have their summer holidays at this time. **March to May** and **September to late October** are quieter and the weather is still warm. From **November to February** you'll find Lisbon emptier, you can wander round the attractions without being bumped from pillar to post, and many of the hotels offer good deals. Over **New Year,** Lisbon fills again for *Reveillon* festivities, so reservations are essential.

Lisbon has become a popular city-break destination in the past few years, as well as hosting large conferences and events at the Feira Internacional de Lisbon (FIL) in Parque das Nações, and at some of the large business hotels with conference facilities. Therefore it is always advisable to reserve ahead to guarantee the hotel and better rates.

Festivals & Special Events

For information and updates on festivals, see www.visitlisboa.com, www.ticketline.pt, or www.whatson when.com.

SPRING. During March, the Half Marathon (www.lisbon-half-marathon. com) starts on the 25 de Abril Bridge, runs up river to Santa Apolónia Station, and back down to Belém. In April, the capital's biggest film festival, IndieLisboa, promotes the cream of new international productions across a range of genres. During May, tennis fans will head to the Estádio Nacional for the **Estoril Open Tennis Championships** (www.estorilopen.net), but tickets are hot property so you might only be able to see the qualifying rounds. At the end of May or beginning of June (depending on when Easter is), Roman Catholics celebrate **Corpus Christi.** There's a solemn parade of priests, religious orders, and the devoted from the Sé (cathedral) in the Alfama through the Baixa. The Holy Sacrament is held by the bishop under a canopy and given an armed guard. You'll see the devotion on some people's faces at the sight of it, with tears streaming down their cheeks.

SUMMER. Everything festival-wise in Lisbon builds up to the **Festas de Lisboa** in June. The main focus is on the city's patron, **St Anthony,** whose saint's day falls on 13th June. The main event takes place the night before, starting with the *Casamentos* or marriages of 12 couples from

Useful Websites

www.visitportugal.com: Turismo de Portugal's official website; it has information on destinations and getting there, plus worldwide contacts.

www.portugaloffice.co.uk: The Portuguese National Tourist Office's official UK website divided into region and holiday type.

www.portugalvirtual.pt: Useful directory with guides, travel information, and tips.

www.cp.pt: The official Portuguese rail website, including schedule and route information, plus online booking.

www.visitlisboa.com: Lisbon's official tourism website with information on attractions, entertainment, tours, transport, accommodation, and restaurants in various languages.

www.estorilcoast.com: Official information on the Estoril coast, including Cascais and Sintra.

different parishes in Lisbon; they drive through the Baixa to the Sé in vintage cars. Later in the evening, the *Marchas Populares* take place, featuring local and international groups performing traditional dances, theatrical performances, and folkloric reenactments along the Avenida da Liberdade. Seating is constructed along the pavement but these are mainly ticketed or reserved for important guests and the press. If you don't fancy squeezing in between for a peek, you can watch it on television at your hotel. Crowds also pour into the Alfama for a concert at the Castelo de São Jorge followed by all-night street parties. Temporary bars are set up in the street and on squares for a month of parties but this is the main night. It's definitely worth battling the crowds. Just watch your wallet and enjoy a plate of sardines and a glass of red wine or sangria, the typical dish and tipple of the night.

The rest of the summer is dominated by music festivals, including the **Sintra Festival of Music and Dance**, the **Estoril Jazz Festival**, and the **Cascais Summer Festival.**

In Lisbon itself, the annual music festival **Superbock Superock** (www.superbock.pt/EN/sbsr.asp) takes over Tejo Park (Parque das Nações) for two weekends in June/July, attracting top bands from Portugal and overseas. Also, Calouste Gulbenkian Foundation hosts **Jazz em Agosto** (www.musica.gulbenkian.pt/jazz) and the **Superliga** soccer season (www.lpfp.pt) starts, giving you an opportunity to see Benfica and Sporting Portugal in action.

FALL. After a hot summer of festivals and music, things get back to business in October with **Moda Lisboa** (www.modalisboa.com), the Portuguese fashion industry's main event, attracting designers and models from around the world. In November, it's the turn of contemporary artists, who come for **Arte Lisboa** (www.artelisboa.fil.pt) at FIL in Parque das Nações.

WINTER. Like its neighbor, Spain, Portugal celebrates **All Saints' Day** (1st November) as a public holiday, a time for remembering relatives and friends who have passed. The cemeteries become a glow of candles as visits are made to place flowers on graves.

To mark the end of the year, Lisbon hosts its own *Reveillon* party at the Torre de Belém. Stages are erected and international musicians invited to play. The concert is free and rounds off with a firework display, but the parties continue through the night in the Bairro Alto.

The winter comes to an end with *Carnaval,* in February, when there's a colorful Brazilian-style parade through the Bairro Alto and plenty of parties late into the night.

The Weather

Lisbon's southerly location means it has a Mediterranean feel, staying pretty warm throughout the year and never extremely cold in winter. Being located at the mouth of the River Tagus, there's an Atlantic breeze relieving the summer heat. During fall and winter the temperature averages around 17.1°C (62.8°F) and the sea is only a couple of degrees cooler than that. There are some beautiful blue-sky days and sometimes you won't even need a jacket, but the city isn't without its rain, so it's always advisable to take a raincoat. By mid-spring, temperatures have risen to an average of 21.8°C (71.2°F), making it pleasant enough to venture along the coast to the beach, and throughout the summer you can expect it to average around 26.3°C (79.3°F)—so take a hat, sunglasses, and plenty of sun cream.

Cellphones (Móviles)

World phones—or GSM (Global System for Mobiles)—work in Portugal (and most of the world). If your cellphone is on a GSM system, and you have a world-capable multiband phone, you can make and receive calls from Portugal. Just call your wireless operator and ask for 'international roaming' to be activated. You can also rent a GSM phone. The French-owned store **FNAC** (main branch at Armázens do Chiado, Rua do Carmo, 2; metro: Baixa-Chiado; ☎ 707-313-435; www.fnac.pt) provides a pay-as-you-go mobile phone package, which could actually be cheaper than renting if you're staying just a few weeks or less. North Americans can rent a GSM phone before leaving home from **InTouch USA** (☎ 800-872-7626; www.intouch global.com) or **RoadPost** (☎ 888-290-1616; www.roadpost.com).

Car Rentals

With so many hills and narrow streets, driving in Lisbon's historic city center is not the most advisable form of transport and relatively few of the hotels here have parking facilities. More hotels in the financial and business district have parking but it's still very busy. However, there are several arterial routes running through Lisbon and out of town, so a car is useful if you're going to explore the Estoril coast or further afield. Remember to take change with you as the motorways charge a toll. Several car hire companies operate from Lisbon's Portela Airport, including **Avis** (☎ 21-843-5550), **Budget** (☎ 21-994-2402), **Europcar** (☎ 21-840-1176), **Hertz** (☎ 21-843-8660), **Nacional/Alamo** (☎ 21-848-6191), and the lesser-known **Auto Jardim** (☎ 21-846-2916) and **Sixt** (☎ 21-847-0661). Most companies can also arrange pick-up at downtown offices or in Cascais and Estoril.

Getting **There**

By Plane

From Lisbon's **Portela** Airport (12km/7 miles from the city center, www.ana.pt), there are several ways to get into town. One is the **Aerobus** Carris service (3.70€ one-day ticket), which leaves from outside the arrivals terminal and stops at Marquês Pombal, Avenida da Liberdade, Praça do Comércio. It operates daily between 7.45am and 8.45pm, departing every 20 minutes and taking approximately 30 minutes. The local bus services nos. 44 and 45 travel to Cais do Sodré, no. 22 to Marques de Pombal, no. 83 to Amoreiras, and no. 5 to Parque das Nações. Tickets can be purchased on board and cost 1.30€.

There is also a **taxi** service operating from the airport. You'll need to pick up a Taxi Voucher from the Tourist Information stand in arrivals. Fares cost around 15€ but this can go up if traffic is heavy. Remember to add 20% for weekends and between the hours of 9pm and 6am, and extra for luggage.

By Car

The **A1** *auto-estrada* or motorway leads to Lisbon from Porto. The **A2** leads to the city from the Algarve, accessible via either the 25 de Abril Bridge downtown or the Vasco da Gama bridge in Parque das Nações. The **A5** runs from the Estoril coast area straight into the city center at Campolide and the **N19** runs between Portela Airport and Sintra. The **A6** links Spain at Badajoz to the **A2** just south of the city, and the **A25** from Salamanca in Spain links with the **A23** then **A1** north of Lisbon. Once you arrive at the city look out for signs to places downtown, including Pombal, Restauradores, and Cais do Sodré, or Parque das Nações and Belém along the river.

By Train

Most long-distance national (Comboios de Portugal; www.cp.pt) and international trains from France and Spain arrive at **Oriente** (Parque das Nações), **Entrecampos** (Avenida das Forcas Armadas), and **Santa Apolónia** (Avenida Infante Dom Henrique; ☎ 808-208-208 (info line); bus: 6, 12, 34). Trains from Estoril and Cascais run along the coast via Belém and terminate at **Cais do Sodré,** and trains from Sintra come into **Entrecampos.**

Getting **Around**

By Metro

The **Metropolitano de Lisboa**—usually known as the metro (☎ 21-350-0115; www.metrolisboa.pt)—is Lisbon's clean and modern subway, and some of its stations are considered works of art as they're covered in Portugal's trademark tiles. The network doesn't cover the whole city but, for the areas where it does run, it's the quickest and easiest way to get around.

You'll need to buy a Viva viagem or 7 colinas (for over seven days) card for .50€, which you'll need to keep for the duration of your stay. You then top the card up with individual, return, day, or weekly fares to the card and 'touch' it on a contact pad as you enter the metro or bus. Single fares cost .80€ for one zone or 1.10€ for two zones. Return fares cost 1.60€ for one zone, 2.20€ for two zones. One-day tickets covering the metro and Carris (bus/tram and lifts, see below) cost 3.70€.

By Taxi

Cream taxis (older ones are black with a turquoise roof) are plentiful and reasonably priced. You can either hail a taxi in the street (the light on the roof means it's available) or grab one where they're lined up (at major squares, such as Rossio and Restauradores). Fares begin at 2€ (2.50€ at night) and baggage costs 1.60€. Reliable taxi companies include **Rádio Taxis** (☎ 21-793-2756), and **Teletáxis** (☎ 21-811-1100). **Tips** are not expected.

By Bus

Buses are operated by Carris, run regularly and go to more places than the metro. However, if it's a choice between the two, the metro is a better option. Most bus routes make their way to the city center to Pombal, Avenida, Restauradores, Praça do Comércio, and Cais do Sodré. There's also a large bus station at Oriente. Carris also operates a night-bus service on eight routes from 11:45pm to 5:30am. Buy your ticket on board or validate your existing

one by touching it on the pad as you board the bus (by the driver).

By Car

Driving through the historic downtown will just frustrate you with its one-way systems, narrow, cobbled streets and hills, as well as lines of traffic and little parking. Even day trips to Sintra, Estoril, and Cascais are less stressful by train. However, if you plan on exploring the Estoril coast, the Sintra Natural Park or south to the Costa da Caparica, then a car is advisable, although the bus network is quite good.

On Foot

Lisbon's city center is best explored on foot but being built on seven hills this is only for fitter travelers. The Baixa is easy as it's flat and even all the way up the Avenida da Liberdade, but you might prefer to take a tram or funicular up to the Alfama, Chiado, and Bairro Alto, and then walk downhill. Belém is flat and pleasant where you can walk through parks and along the riverfront, but building work may mean walking along the busy Avenida da Brasília. The Parque das Nações is also pleasant to walk around as it's mainly pedestrianized, but again you can combine it with the cable car, tourist train, and cycle hire.

Fast **Facts**

APARTMENT RENTALS Lisbon rental options include: **LisbonNet** (☎ 917-711-658; www.lisbonet.com), which has apartments in the Bairro Alto; **www.holiday-lettings.co.uk/lisbon**, with everything from basic apartments to luxury houses available for short-term lets in the city center and environs; and **onlyapartments** (www.only-apartments.com), which offers rentals for both short

and longer periods throughout the city center.

ATMS/CASHPOINTS Maestro, Cirrus, and Visa cards are readily accepted at all ATMs. Exchange currency either at banks, automatic currency exchange machines, or *casas de câmbio* (bureaux de change). There are currency exchange offices in both arrivals and departures at Portela

Airport. Portuguese banks include the Banco de Portugal, Banco Espírito Santo e Comercial (BES), Banif, BPI, Credito Agrícola, and Millennium BCP. There are branches with ATMs throughout the city center, particularly in the Chiado, Baixa, Avenida da Liberdade, Saldanha, and Amoreiras. You'll also find ATMs in all the shopping centers.

BUSINESS HOURS Banks are open Monday through Friday from 8:30am to 3pm. Most offices are open Monday through Friday from 9am to 6 or 7pm. At restaurants, lunch is usually from 12pm or 12:30pm to 2:30pm or 3pm and dinner from 7pm or 7:30pm to 10pm or 10:30pm. Shops generally open Monday to Friday 9am or 10am and close at 7pm. Some close from 1–3pm during the week and in the Chiado/Baixa some stay open till 8pm or 9pm. Major shopping centers stay open until midnight every day.

CONSULATES & EMBASSIES **US Embassy**, Avenida das Forças Armadas (☎ 21 727 3300, portugal. usembassy.gov); **Canadian Embassy**, Avenida da Liberdade, 196–200, 3rd floor (☎ 21-316-4600, www.canadainternational.gc.ca); **UK Embassy**, Rua de São Bernardo, 33 (☎ 21-392-4000, ukinportugal. fco.gov.uk/en); **Australian Embassy**, Avenida da Liberdade, 196–200, 2nd floor (☎ 21-310-1500, www.portugal.embassy.gov. au); **New Zealand Consulate**, Rua do Periquito, Lote A-13, Quinta da Bicuda, Cascais (☎ 21-370-5779). **South African Embassy**, Avenida Luís Bívar, 10 (☎ 21-319-2200).

DOCTORS Dial ☎ 112 in an emergency.

ELECTRICITY Most hotels operate on 220/380 volts AC (50 hertz). Plugs are European Standard. To use an American-style plug, you'll need a 220-volt transformer and adapter plug.

EMERGENCIES For an ambulance or medical emergencies, fire or police, call ☎ 112.

GAY & LESBIAN TRAVELERS In 1982, 7 years after the end of the Salazar dictatorship, Portugal decriminalized homosexuality in private among consenting adults. In 1995, it adjusted the law on crimes related to sexuality to reflect individual right to sexual freedom. Due to the strong influence of the Roman Catholic Church on Portuguese society, further legislation was slow to pass, but cohabiting couples were given some rights of marriage from 2001, and in 2004 the constitution banned discrimination on the basis of sexual orientation. Although this still meant same-sex couples could not marry, in January 2010 a bill was passed backing it and at the time of writing it looked like gay marriage would be legalized. Gay rights' groups are active in Portugal, the largest of which is ILGA-Portugal (www.ilga-portugal.oninet.pt), which has helped organize events such as Gay Pride and Gay and Lesbian Film Festivals. There are also various gay bars and clubs in Lisbon (see p. 120).

HOLIDAYS Public holidays observed include: 1 January (New Year's Day), February (Mardi Gras/Carnival), March/April (Good Friday and Easter Monday), 25 April (Liberty Day—Carnation Revolution), 1 May (May Day), May (Corpus Christi), 10 June (National Day), 13 June (St Anthony's Day), 15 August (Feast of the Assumption), 5 October (Republic Day), 1 November (All Saints' Day), 1 December (Restoration of Independence Day), 8 December (Feast of the Immaculate Conception), and 25 December (Christmas).

INSURANCE You should check any existing insurance policies, making sure you purchase any necessary additional travel insurance to cover cancellations, lost luggage, theft, medical expenses, and car rental insurance. For more information, contact one of the following insurers: **Access America** (☎ 800-284-8300; www.accessamerica.com); **Travel Guard International** (☎ 800-826-4919; www.travelguard.com); **Travel Insured International** (☎ 800-243-3174; www.travelinsured.com); and **Travelex Insurance Services** (☎ 800-228-9792; www.travelex-insurance.com). For travel overseas, most US health plans (including Medicare and Medicaid) do not provide coverage, and the ones that do often require payment for services upfront. If you require additional medical insurance, try **MEDEX Assistance** (☎ 800-537-2029; www.medexassist.com) or **Travel Assistance International** (☎ 800-821-2828; www.travelassistance.com).

INTERNET Internet access is becoming easy to find, from hotel lobbies (which regularly offer Wi-Fi) to cybercafes (cafés Internet). There are also a lot of Internet cafes and access points. **Lisbon Welcome Center** in Praça do Comércio has several terminals. Other places include Mar Adentro Café at Rua do Alecrim, 35; Cyber.Bica at Rua dos Duques de Bragança, 7, www.cyberbica.com; and Cineteka, Avda do Mediterraneo, Lt 1.02., www.cineteka.com.

LOST PROPERTY You should call credit card companies as soon as you discover your wallet has been lost or stolen and file a report at the nearest police station. Your credit card company may require a police report number or record. **American Express** cardholders and travelers'

check holders should call ☎ 21-427-0400 (US) or ☎+44 1273 571 600 (UK) in Portugal. **Diners Club** emergency numbers are ☎ 21-315-9856 (US) and ☎ +44 1 252 513 500 (UK) in Portugal. **MasterCard** holders should call ☎ 800-811-272 in Portugal. **Visa** emergency number is ☎ 800-811-107 in Portugal.

MAIL & POSTAGE Portuguese post offices are called correios (koh-ray-os), identified by red signs with a white logo depicting a man on a horse playing a bugle and the word Correios below. Main offices are generally open from Mon–Fri 9am–6pm, but the main post office in Praça dos Restauradores (☎ 21-323-8971) is open Mon–Fri 8am–10pm, Sat and Sun 9am–6pm. Other branches are at the Centro Cultural de Belém (Praça do Império), Campo Pequeno (Rua Arco do Cego, 88), and the airport (24-hour service).

MONEY The single European currency in Portugal is the **euro** (€), divided into 100 cents. At press time, the exchange rate was approximately 1€ = \$1.41 or £0.70. For up-to-the-minute exchange rates between the euro and the dollar, check the currency converter website **www.xe.com**.

PASSPORTS US, Canadian, Australian, and New Zealand visitors to Portugal do not need a visa if their stay does not exceed 90 days. South African visitors do need a visa. If your passport is lost or stolen, contact your country's embassy or consulate immediately. See 'Consulates & Embassies' above. You should make a copy of your passport's critical pages and keep it separate from the original.

PHARMACIES Pharmacies (farmacias) operate from Mon–Fri 9am–1pm and 3–7pm and Saturday mornings. There are also 24-hour pharmacies, which follow a schedule displayed in the window. To find a pharmacy near you, call ☎ 800-202-134.

POLICE The national police emergency number is ☎ 112. For local police, call ☎ 21-321-7000.

SAFETY Lisbon doesn't have a high violent crime rate compared to many other cities, but there has been a rise in incidents in the past couple of decades. It's generally safe to walk around Lisbon even at night but you should be cautious in parts of the Alfama and Bairro Alto, particularly narrow streets where it's quieter and not so well lit. Just don't walk alone or make sure you take a taxi back to your hotel. Most establishments will be happy to call one for you. Also watch your belongings on Tram 28, which is renowned for pickpockets. Almost everyday someone loses something because they're too busy looking out of the window. You don't have to miss out on the attractions. Just hold onto your wallet and watch, or put your bag at the front where you can see it, and you shouldn't have a problem. If you are unlucky enough to be a victim of crime, there's a dedicated Tourism Police office at Palácio Foz (the same building as the Tourist Office) in Praça dos Restauradores (☎ 21-342-1634).

SMOKING On 1 January, 2008, Portugal introduced a smoking ban in enclosed spaces in public places and commercial establishments. However, proprietors of spaces larger than 100m2 can choose to allow or prohibit smoking, but they must make display signs and provide designated smoking areas with air conditioning. ANA, the Portuguese airport authority followed by announcing a full ban on smoking in public areas at all airports except Lisbon, where there are designated smoking areas.

TAXES The value-added (VAT) tax (known in Portugal as IVA) ranges from 5% to 20%, depending on the commodity being sold. Food, wine, and basic necessities are taxed at 5%; most goods and services (including car rentals and restaurant meals) at 12%; luxury items (jewelry, all tobacco, imported liquors) at 21%; and hotels at 5%. Non-EU residents are entitled to a reimbursement of the 20% IVA tax on most purchases worth more than 60.35 € made at shops offering 'Tax Free' or 'Global Refund' shopping. You should ask the store for a declaration form when you purchase the item(s), detailing the amount paid, the amount bought, and the amount to be reimbursed. You can claim the reimbursement at the airport in cash, by credit card, or international check, but you must show the items in question to the Customs officials beforehand. For more information see www.premiertaxfree.com and www.portugaltaxrefund.com.pt.

TELEPHONES For national telephone information, dial ☎ 118. For international telephone information, dial ☎ 177. If you want to make an international call, dial ☎ 00 followed by the country code, area code, and number. If you're making a local or long-distance call in Portugal, dial the two-digit city code first (**21** in the Lisbon area) followed by the seven-digit number. Public phones take coins or phone-cards, which can be bought at the post office or *tabacaria* (newsagent) booths. You can also make calls from phone booths at post offices.

TIPPING Menu prices should usually include the 12% service charge. Leaving a tip is discretionary but in more expensive restaurants and tourist areas a tip of 5% to 10% is becoming more common. For coffees and snacks you don't need to tip, although some people leave a few small coins. Taxis do not expect tips but you should tip hotel porters, doormen, and maids 1€ per day.

TOILETS In Portugal they're called *casas de banho* or *lavabos*, and are labeled *homens* for men and *senhoras* for women.

TOURIST INFORMATION **Lisbon Welcome Center**, Praça do Comércio (☎ 21-031-2810), is open daily 9am to 8pm. There are other Turismo de Portugal offices or kiosks at **Palácio Foz**, Praça dos Restauradores (☎ 21-346-3314); **Aeroporto de Portela**, Arrivals Hall (☎ 21-845-0660); **Estação de Santa Apolónia**, International Terminal (☎ 21-882-1606); **Rua Augusta**, Baixa (☎ 21-325-9131); and a kiosk by the **Mosteiro dos Jerónimos**, Belém (☎ 21-365-8435).

TOURS Cityline/Sightline (☎ 21-343-1405; www.cityline-sightline.pt) operates hop-on, hop-off bus tours around the city, with 13 stops close to major attractions. Tickets cost 15€ for 1 day and 22€ for 2-day tickets (children 7.50€ and 11€). Buses start at Praça de Pombal and also pass Rossio Square, Praça de Comércio, Cais do Sodré, and Belém. They also operate out-of-town tours to the Estoril coast and Fatima.

TRAVELERS WITH DISABILITIES Portugal has been coming in line with EU regulations and many modern hotels now have ramps and lifts, and there are also lifts at most main stations on the metro. There are disabled parking spaces and lifts at the airport, and assistance is also available, but you need to request this at the time of booking. **Accessible Portugal** (☎ 21-720-3130; www.accessibleportugal.com) offers escorted tours, mainly operating out of Lisbon.

Lisbon: **A Brief History**

205 B.C. Romans form a municipality in Lisbon, naming it *Felicitus Julia*.

5TH–6TH C. A.D. German tribes occupy the city, including the Vandals and the Visigoths, calling it *Ulishbona*.

711 Moors (Muslims from north Africa) arrive on the Iberian peninsula, taking Lisbon (*Al-Ushbuna*) 3 years later, building a fortress on top of the Al-Hamma (Alfama).

1147 Dom Afonso Henriques takes the city, helped by crusaders, including the Order of Christ. He orders the building of the Sé (cathedral) on top of the mosque.

12TH–13TH C. Commercial links with north Africa improve and those in professions linked to navigation (carpenters and sailors) are given special privileges.

1256 Dom Afonso III moves his court to Lisbon and makes it the new capital of the country.

1290 Dom Dinis creates the first university in Lisbon but moves it to Coimbra in 1308.

1308 Portugal makes its first commercial treaty with England.

1383–5 Dom Fernando I dies without an heir, leaving way for João of Castille (Dom João I) to become king, but civil war and disease reign for two years.

1386 The Treaty of Windsor reinforces the Anglo–Portuguese alliance, along with the marriage between Dom João I and Philippa of Lancaster.

1415 The Infante Dom Henrique (Prince Henry the Navigator) conquers Ceuta, heralding the Golden Age of Discovery.

1487 Bartolomeu Dias rounds the Cape of Good Hope.

1498 Vasco da Gama reaches India, providing a new spice route and other commercial activity.

1500 Pedro Alvares Cabral arrives in Bahia (Brazil).

1501 Work begins on the Mosteiro dos Jerónimos, ordered by Dom Manuel I and in the Manueline style named after him.

1540 The first *auto da fé* takes place in Rossio Square, the public trial and massacre of people of Jewish heritage.

1572 Luis Vaz de Camões's epic poem of history and maritime discovery, *Os Lusadas* (The Lusiads), is first published.

1580 Two years after Dom Sebastião dies without an heir, Dom Felipe I (Felipe II of Spain) is crowned king.

1640 Following the War of Restoration, the Duque de Bragança (Dom João IV) takes the throne, and the old commercial alliance with England is reinstated.

17TH–18TH C. Gold discovered in Brazil is used to build luxurious palaces and convents.

1755 An earthquake and subsequent tsunami, fires, and disease devastate Lisbon, killing around 10,000 people.

LATE 18TH C. Marquês de Pombal, Prime Minister to Dom José I, rebuilds the city, which brings new commercial activity.

1807 Napoleonic troops enter the city, but it is retaken a year later with the help of the English.

1822 Brazil wins independence and Dom Pedro I becomes the first emperor.

19TH C. Civil wars over accession to the throne.

1836 The old Inquisition House in Rossio is demolished, due to campaigning by writer Almeida Garrett, and the Teatro Dona Maria II is built in its place.

1856–70 First railway line is built between Lisbon and Carregado, followed by lines to Porto and the building of Santa Apolónia and Rossio stations.

1878 Electricity comes to Lisbon and the first lifts up the hills are installed around 1880.

1886 Avenida da Liberdade is constructed.

1910 Revolution and declaration of the First Republic.

1914–17 Portugal joins the allies during the First World War.

1918 Spanish flu kills thousands.

1926–33 First Republic ends and a military dictatorship rules.

1933–74 Semi-fascist *Novo Estado* (New State) imposed by António de Oliveira de Salazar.

1935 Writer Fernando Pessoa dies of a hepatic ulcer.

1960 Padrão dos Descobrimentos rebuilt to commemorate the 500th anniversary of the death of Henry the Navigator.

1966 Ponte Salazar, a bridge across the Tagus River, is inaugurated, later renamed Ponte 25 de Abril.

1974 On 25th April, the peaceful Carnation Revolution takes power.

1975 First democratic elections in 50 years won by the Social Democrat Party.

1986 Portugal joins the EU.

1992 The Centro Cultural de Belém is inaugurated.

1994 Lisbon is European Capital of Culture, attracting visitors and international attention.

1998 Lisbon hosts Expo '98 in the newly built Parque das Nações.

2004 Portugal hosts the European soccer championships, with the final taking place at Lisbon's Estádio da Luz.

2010 Portugal legalizes same-sex marriages.

Useful Phrases

Useful Words & Phrases

NUMBER	PORTUGUESE	PRONUNCIATION
Good day	Bom dia	bom-dee-ah
How are you?	Como está?	kohm shtah
Very well	Muito bem	moy-to bey-m
Thank you	Obrigado/a	o-bree-gah-doh /dah
You're welcome	De nada	deh nah-dah
Goodbye	Adeus	ah-day-oosh
Please	Por favor/Faz favor	por fah-vohr/fash fah-vohr
Yes	Sim	si-(m)
No	Não	now
Excuse me	Desculpe	deh-shkoolp
Where is . . . ?	Onde fica ...?	ohn-day fee-kah...?
To the right	À direito	ah deer-eh-toh
To the left	À esquerda	ah esh-kair-dah
I would like . . .	Eu gostaria...	eh-ooh gosh-tah-ree-ya
I want . . .	Quero...	kair-roh...
Do you have . . . ?	Tem?	Tay-m?
How much is it?	Quanto é?/	kwahn-toh eh?/
	Quanto custa?	kwahn-toh coosh-tah?
When?	Quando?	kwahn-doh?
What?	Como? / O qué?	Coh-moh? / oh-keh?
There is (Is there . . . ?)	Ha . . . ?	aye/ee ah/ee ahn
Yesterday	Ontem	ohn-tey-m
Today	Hoje	ohj
Tomorrow	Amanha	ah-mah-nyah-ah
Good	Bom	boh-m
Bad	Mau	m-owh
Better (Best)	(O) melhor	(oh) meh-ly-ohr
More	Mais	my-sh
Less	Menos	meh-nohs/meh-nyus

NUMBER	PORTUGUESE	PRONUNCIATION
Do you speak English?	Fala inglês?	Fah-lah eeng-gleysh?
I speak a	Falo um pouco	Fah-loh oom poh-koh
little Portuguese	de português	day port-you-qeysh
I don't understand	Não percebo	now pair-seb-oh
What time is it?	Qué horas são?	keh oh-rahsh s-owh
The check, please	À conta, faz favor	ah con-tah fash fah-vohr
The station	À estação	ah es-tah-saoh
a hotel	um hotel	oom oh-tehl
the market	o mercado	oh mehr-kah-doh
restaurant	um restaurante	oom rehs-tow-rahnt
the toilet	o lavabo	oh lah-vah-boh
a doctor	um médico	oon meh-dee-koh
the road to . . .	a estrada	ah esh-trah-dah
to eat	comer	ko-mehr
a room	um cuarto	oom quah-toh
a book	um livro	oom lee-vroh
a dictionary	um diccionario	oom dik-syoh-nah-ryoh

Numbers

NUMBER	PORTUGUESE	PRONUNCIATION
1	um	oom
2	dois	doysh
3	três	tresh
4	cuatro	kwah-troh
5	cinco	sink-oh
6	seis	saysh
7	sete	set
8	oito	oy-toh
9	nove	nov
10	dez	desh
11	onze	onz
12	doze	doz
13	treze	treh-z
14	catorze	kah-tohr-z
15	quinze	kin-z
16	dezaseis	dez-ah-saysh
17	dezasete	dez-ah-set
18	dezoito	dez-oy-to
19	dezanove	dez-ah-nov
20	vinte	vint
30	trinta	trin-tah
40	quarenta	kwah-rehn-tah
50	cinquenta	sing-kwehn-tah
60	sessenta	seh-sehn-tah
70	setenta	seh-tehn-tah
80	oitenta	oy-tehn-tah
90	noventa	noh-behn-tah
100	cem	cey-m

Index

See also Accommodations and Restaurant indexes, below.

A

Accessory stores, 85–86
Accommodations. See also
    Accommodations Index
    best bets, 132
    maps, 133–137
    reservations, 140
    types of lodging, 139
Adega Mesquita, 119
Airports, 165
Alameda dos Oceanos, 32
Alfama neighborhood,
    3, 4, 52–57
Alfama streets, 53
All Saints' Day, 163–164
A Loja de Artesano, 66
Alternative music venues,
    122
Alto dos Moinhos station, 50
Amoreiras neighborhood,
    74–76
Amoreiras shopping
    center, 31
Antiques, 82
Apartment rentals, 166
Architecture, 22–29
    Assembleia da
        República, 76
    Eden Teatro, 59
    Igreja de Santa Engrácia
        e Panteão Nacional,
        23–24, 36, 37
    Manueline, 4, 11–13,
        24, 28, 39, 65, 70–72
    Pavilhão de Portugal,
        18, 20, 28–29
    Pre-Reconquest, 23
Arco de São Jorge, 53–54
Arco do Triunfo (Triumph
    Arch), 3, 7, 25, 62–63
Art, outdoor, 20
Arte Lisboa, 163
Art galleries and museums,
    44–50, 82
    Campo de Ourique, 75
    Centro Cultural de
        Belém, 14
    Centro de Arte Moderna José Acervedo
        Perdigão, 48–49
    Museu Calouste Gulbenkian, 16–17, 48

Museu Colecção Berardo
    de Arte Moderna e
    Contemporânea,
    14, 46–47, 71
Museu de Arte
    Moderno, 160
Museu do Chiado, 47–48
Museu Nacional de Arte
    Antiga, 17, 45
Museu Nacional do
    Azulejo (National Tile
    Museum), 49–50
Museu National de Arte
    Antiga (MNAC), 10
Parque das Nações, 20
Arts centers, 129
    Chapitô, 124, 129
    Culturgest, 124, 129
Ascensor da Bica, 67
Assembleia da República, 76
ATMs, 166–167
Avenida da Liberdade,
    27–28, 59–60
Avenida-Parque neighbor-
    hood, 58–61
Azulejos (tiles), 49
Azurara Palace, 54

B

Bacon, Francis, 46
Bairro Alto neighborhood,
    3, 66–69
Baixa, 3, 9, 25, 62–65
Bar 106, 120
Bars and pubs
    Bar 106, 120
    Bar Terraço, 116
    Belém Café Bar, 116
    Catacumbas Jazz
        Bar, 121
    Cinco Lounge, 112, 118
    Comida da Ribeira, 66
    Enoteca de Belém, 122
    Ginjinha do Rossio,
        65, 112, 116–117
    Hennessey's Irish
        Pub, 117
    Hot Clube de
        Portugal, 121
    Incognito Bar, 122
    Irish & Co., 117
    Lux Bar & Club, 119
    Mezcal, 112, 117
    Onda Jazz, 121
    Op Art Café, 118
    O Terraço, 4, 112, 117
    Peter Café Sport, 117
    Solar do Vinho do
        Porto, 43, 112, 122
    Speakeasy Bar, 121–122

Bar Terraço, 116
Basilica da Estrela, 9, 75
Beaches, 33, 148–149
Belém, 70–73, 94–96
Belém Café Bar, 116
Belém Cultural Center
    (CCB), 46
Berardo Collection of Contemporary and Modern
    Art, 14, 46–47, 71
Bicycling, 4, 18, 32
Blues Café dance club, 118
Boating, 33, 41, 153
Boca do Inferno, 152
The Book of Disquiet
    (Fernando Pessoa), 36
Book stores, 82
Botanic Gardens (Jardim
    Botânico), 3–4, 42–43,
    69, 93
Buses, 166
Business hours, 87, 167

C

Cable cars, 18–19, 32
Cabral, Pedro Alvares, 11
Café Luso, 119
Cais do Sodré neighborhood,
    66–69, 72
Cais do Sodré train station,
    165
Calatrava, Santiago (architect), 29
Camping, 96
Campo de Ourique, 75
Campo Grande station, 50
Capas Negras, 36
Capela de Nossa Senhora de
    Saúde, 52
Carcavelos beach, 149
Carnation Revolution, 29, 35
Carnaval, 164
Car rentals, 164
Cartão do Parque (Park
    Card), 18
Casa de Santa Marta,
    152–153
Casa do Ferreiro das
    Tabuletas, 26
Casa dos Bicos, 24, 25,
    57, 157
Casa dos Tapetes de
    Arraiolos, 69
Casamentos, 162, 163
Casa-Museu Amália
    Rodrigues, 76
Cascais, 149, 150–155
Cascais Summer Festival, 163
Cashpoints, 166–167
Casino do Estoril,
    117, 154–155

Casino Lisboa, 20, 117–118
Castelo de São Jorge, 3, 4, 8, 37, 41–42, 53–54, 163
Castelo dos Mouros, 157–158
Catacumbas Jazz Bar, 121
Cathedrals. see Churches and cathedrals
Cavalho e Melo, Sebastião José, 36, 37
CCB (Belém Cultural Center), 46
Cellphones, 164
Centro Cultural de Belém, 14, 71, 73, 124, 127, 128
Centro de Arte Moderna Jose Acervedo Perdigão, 48–49
Centro Vasco da Gama, 19, 20
Ceramics, 83
Chanel, Coco, 47
Chapitô art center, 124, 129
Chiado neighborhood, 66–69
Children, activities for, 30–33
    beaches and boating, 33, 41
    historical sites and history museums, 14, 28, 33, 71–72, 95
    parks and gardens, 32–33, 93, 95
    restaurants, 105
    science and math museums, 17, 31
    in Sintra, 33
    trains, trams, and cable cars, 7–8, 18–19, 32
Churches and cathedrals
    Basilica da Estrela, 9, 75
    Capela de Nossa Senhora de Saúde, 52
    Convento do Carmo, 68
    Igreja de Santa Engrácia e Panteão Nacional, 23–24, 36, 37, 55
    Igreja de Santa Luzia e São Bras, 8, 54–56
    Igreja de Santo António de Lisboa, 37, 38, 56
    Igreja de São Roque, 26–27
    Igreja do Convento do Carmo, 26
    Mosteiro de São Vicente de Fora, 54, 55
    Mosteiro dos Jerónimos, 4, 11–12, 28, 39, 70–73
    Sé (Cathedral), 8–9, 23, 56
Cidadela, 154

Cinco Lounge, 112, 118
Cinema de São Jorge, 60, 128
Cinema Londres, 124, 128
Cinemas, 19, 20, 31, 60, 124, 128, 129
Cinemateca, 124, 128
City Center gardens, 92–93
Classical music venues, 127–128
Climate, 162, 164
Clube de Fado, 112, 119–120
Clube VII fitness club, 91
Club Souk dance club, 118
Cocktail bars, 118
Coliseu dos Recreios, 124, 127
Columbo shopping center, 31
Comida da Ribeira bar, 66
Consulates, 167
Convento do Carmo, 4, 9, 64, 68
Corpus Christi celebration, 162
Costa, António, 49
Costa do Estoril beach hopping, 148–149
Cristo do Rei statue, 33, 35, 41
Culturgest art center, 124, 129
Currency, 168
Cycle of the Masters (Willem van der Kloet), 49

D
Dali, Salvador, 46
Dance clubs, 112, 118–119
Dance performances, 128
Day trips and excursions, 148–160
    Cascais and Estoril, 150–155
    Costa do Estoril, 148–149
    Sintra, 156–160
de Almeida, Leopoldo, 15
Delaunay, Robert, 48
Delaunay, Sonia, 48
de Matos, Marçal, 49
Department stores, 83, 84
Dias, Bartolomeu, 11
Dining. See also Restaurant Index
    best bets, 98
    maps, 31, 99–101
    at shopping centers, 31
Disabilities, travelers with, 170
Discoveries Monument (Padrão dos Descobrimentos), 15, 39, 73

Doctors, 167
dos Santos, Bartolomeu Cid, 50
Dragão do Alfama, 120
Driving, 153, 158, 165, 166
Duchamp, Marcel, 46

E
Eden Teatro, 28, 59
Electricity, 167
Elevador de Santa Justa, 9, 25, 63–64
Embassies, 167
Emergencies, 167
Enoteca de Belém, 112, 122
Entertainment. See Performing arts and entertainment
Entrecampos station, 50, 165
Ernst, Max, 46
Estação do Oriente, 29
Estádio da Luz, 129–130
Estádio José de Alvalade, 130
Estádio Nacional, 130, 162
Estoril, 149, 150–155
Estoril Jazz Festival, 163
Estoril Open Tennis Championships, 162
Estrela neighborhood, 74–76
Estufas, in Parque Eduardo VII, 91
Exploratorium, 31

F
Fado music, 3, 36, 119–120
    Adega Mesquita, 119
    Café Luso, 119
    Clube de Fado, 119–120
    Dragão do Alfama, 120
    Museu do Fado, 36
    Timpanas, 120
Fashion stores, 85–86
Feira da Ladra market, 3, 84
Feira do Livro book festival, 60
Fernão de Magalhães, 11
Festas de Lisboa, 162
Festivals, 162–164
Film. See Cinemas
Follow Me Lisboa event guide, 129
Frágil dance club, 118
Fringe arts centers, 129
Full-day tours, 6–20
    one day, 6–9
    two days, 10–15
    three days, 16–20
Fundação Calouste Gulbenkian, 124
Furniture stores, 84–85

G

Garcia Horta Gardens, 19
Gardens
    Assembleia da
        República, 76
    García Horta Gardens, 19
    Jardim Amália
        Rodrigues, 61, 91
    Jardim Botânico
        (Botanic Gardens),
        3–4, 42–43, 69, 93
    Jardim Botânico
        d'Ajuda, 95
    Jardim da Estrela, 93
    Jardim da Fundação
        Calouste Gulbenkian,
        93
    Jardim do Principe
        Real, 93
    Jardim do Ultramar,
        70, 95–96
    Museau Calouste
        Gulbenkian, 16–17,
        48–49
    Palacio Nacional do
        Queluz, 160
    Parque Eduardo VII,
        91–96
    Quinta da Regaleira,
        159–160
    Tagus Gardens Park, 33
Gay and lesbian travelers,
    112, 120–121, 167
Gehry, Frank O., 47
Gifts, 86
Ginjinha do Rosslo bar,
    112, 116–117
Givenchy, 47
Go-kart rentals, 32
Golfing, 155
Gonçalves, Nuno, 45
Gorky, Arshile, 49
Gormley, Antony, 20, 49
Gossip club, 120
Gourmet food and drink
    stores, 86–87
Grande e Pequeno Audito-
    rio: Calouste Gulbenkian
    Foundation, 127
Greenhouses, in Parque
    Eduardo VII, 91
Guincho, 149
Gulbenkian, Calouste Sarkis,
    16–17, 48

H

Half Marathon, 162
Hard Rock Café, 122
Hennessey's Irish Pub,
    112, 117
Henriques, Dom Afonso, 37

Henry the Navigator, 11, 39
Historical sites and muse-
    ums. *See also* Churches
    and cathedrals; Palaces
    Arco de São Jorge,
        53–54
    Casa de Santa Marta,
        152–153
    Casa dos Bicos, 24, 25,
        57, 157
    Cidadela, 154
    Convento do Carmo,
        4, 9, 64, 68
    Elevador de Santa Justa,
        9, 25, 63–64
    Mosteiro de São Vicente
        de Fora, 54, 55
    Museu Arqueológico,
        9, 68
    Museu da Marinha, 13
    Museu do Teatro
        Romano, 23, 56
    Museum of Decorative
        Arts (Museu de Artes
        Decorativas), 50, 52,
        54, 55
    Museu Municipal de
        Cascais, 152
    Museu Nacional de
        Arqueologia, 13
    Museu Nacional de
        História Nacional, 42
    Rossio Square, 9, 64–65
    Torre de Belém, 4, 14,
        28, 71–72, 96, 164
Holidays, 162, 167
Home goods stores, 84–85
Homen—Sol (Jorge Viera), 20
Hot Clube de Portugal,
    112, 121

I

ICEP Portugal–Portuguese
    Trade and Tourism Office,
    162
Igreja de Santa Engrácia e
    Panteão Nacional, 23–24,
    36, 37, 55
Igreja de Santa Luzia e São
    Bras, 8, 54–56
Igreja de Santo António de
    Lisboa, 37, 38, 56
Igreja de São Roque, 26–27
Igreja do Convento do
    Carmo, 26
Incognito Bar, 122
Indie Lisboa film festival, 162
Infante Dom Henrique, 11, 39
Insurance, 168
Internet, 168
Irish & Co. pub, 117

J

Jardim Amália Rodrigues,
    61, 91
Jardim Botânico (Botanic
    Gardens), 3–4, 42–43,
    69, 93
Jardim Botânico d'Ajuda, 95
Jardim da Estrela, 93
Jardim da Fundação Calo-
    uste Gulbenkian, 93
Jardim do Principe Real, 93
Jardim do Ultramar,
    70, 95–96
Jardim Zoológico de Lisboa,
    32–33, 95
Jazz bars, 121–122
Jazz em Agosto festival, 163
Jewelry stores, 87
Jewish Quarter, 57

K

Knowledge Pavilion (Pavil-
    hão de Conhecimento),
    17, 31

L

Laranjeiras station, 50
Largo das Portas do Sol, 54
Largo do Rato, 74
Largo Luis de Camões, 38
Largo Martim Moniz, 52
Leather goods stores, 88
Lisboa Card, 61
Lisboa No Bolsa event
    guide, 129
Lisbon
    favorite moments in,
        2–4
    history of, 170–172
Lisbon exhibition center, 19
Lisbon's heroes tour,
    34–39
Lisbon Welcome Center,
    3, 7, 61, 96, 129, 140,
    168, 170
Live Mathematics, 31
The Loft dance club, 119
Lost property, 168
Luis de Camões, 36–38,
    67–68
Lusomundo, 124, 128, 129
Lux Bar & Club, 112, 119

M

Magellan, Ferdinand, 11
Mail, 168
Manuel I, Dom, 24
Manueline architecture,
    4, 11–13, 24, 28, 39,
    65, 70–72

Manuel Tavares wine shop, 64
Marchas Populares festival, 163
Marina de Cascais, 153
Maritime exploration, 11
Markets, 3, 66–67, 75, 84
Mata de São Domingos de Benfica, 95
Maternidade (Carlos Botero), 91
Mercado da Ribeira, 66–67
Mesnier de Ponsard, Raul, 25
Message (Fernando Pessoa), 36
Metro, 18, 50, 165–166
Mezcal bar, 112, 117
Mini-train, 32
Miradouro de Santa Luzia, 8, 42, 54, 55
Miradouro de São Pedro de Alcântara, 68–69
Miradouros, 4
MNAC (Museu Nacional de Arte Antiga), 10, 17, 45
Mobile phones, 164
Moda Lisboa, 163
Money, 168
Monstros Marinhos (Pedro Proença), 20
Monumento Cristo Rei, 41
Mosteiro de São Vicente de Fora, 54, 55
Mosteiro dos Jerónimos, 4, 11–12, 28, 39, 70–73
Móviles, 164
MuDe (Museum of Fashion and Design), 47, 63
Museu Arqueológico, 9, 68
Museu Calouste Gulbenkian, 16–17, 48
Museu Colecção Berardo de Arte Moderna e Contemporânea, 14, 46–47, 71
Museu da Marinha, 13
Museu da Marioneta, 46
Museu da Musica, 154
Museu das Comunicações, 46
Museu de Arte Moderno, 160
Museu de Artes Decorativas (Museum of Decorative Arts), 50, 52, 54, 55
Museu do Brinquedo, 160
Museu do Chiado, 47–48
Museu do Fado, 36
Museu do Teatro Romano, 23, 56
Museum of Decorative Arts (Museu de Artes Decorativas), 50, 52, 54, 55

Museum of Fashion and Design (MuDe), 47, 63
Museu Municipal de Cascais, 152
Museu Nacional de Arqueologia, 13
Museu Nacional de Arte Antiga (MNAC), 10, 17, 45
Museu Nacional de História Nacional, 42
Museu Nacional do Azulejo (National Tile Museum), 26, 49–50
Music, 14, 33, 88, 127–128
Music Playground, 33

N

National Tile Museum (Museu Nacional do Azulejo), 26, 49–50
Nations' Park (Parque das Nações), 20, 29, 32, 33
Neighborhood walks, 52–76
  Alfama, 52–57
  Avenida-Parque, 58–61
  Baixa, 62–65
  Belém neighborhood, 70–73
  Cais do Sodré, Chiado and Bairro Alto, 66–69
  Rato, Amoreiras and Estrela, 74–76
Nery, Eduardo, 50
Nightlife, 112–122
  bars and pubs, 116–117
  best bets, 112
  casinos, 117–118
  cocktail bars, 118
  dance clubs, 112, 118–119
  fado, 119–120
  gay and lesbian, 120–121
  jazz bars, 121–122
  maps, 113–116
  rock and alternative venues, 122
  wine and port bars, 122

O

Oceanário, 17–19, 31
Onda Jazz, 121
Op Art Café, 118
Order of Malta, 42
Oriente train station, 18, 50, 165
Os Lusíadas (Luis Vaz de Camões), 38
O Terraço bar, 4, 112, 117

Outdoor activities, 90–96
  City Center gardens, 92–93
  Parque Eduardo VII, 90–91
  Parque Florestal de Monsanto & Belém, 94–96
Outdoor art, 20

P

Padrão dos Descobrimentos (Discoveries Monument), 15, 39, 73
Painel de Nossa Senhora da Vida (Marçal de Matos), 49
Palaces
  Azurara Palace, 54
  Museu de Artes Decorativas (Museum of Decorative Arts), 50, 52, 54, 55
  Museu Municipal de Cascais, 152
  Palácio da Foz, 28, 59
  Palácio de Belém, 70
  Palácio dos Marqueses da Fronteira, 95
  Palacio Nacional da Pena, 157
  Palacio Nacional de Queluz, 160
  Palacio Nacional de Sintra, 158, 159
  Royal Palace, 53
Palácio da Foz, 28, 59
Palácio de Belém, 70
Palácio dos Marqueses da Fronteira, 95
Palácio Nacional da Pena, 157
Palácio Nacional de Queluz, 160
Palácio Nacional de Sintra, 158, 159
Park Card (Cartão do Parque), 18
Parks
  Mata de São Domingos de Benfica, 95
  Miradouro de São Pedro de Alcântara, 68–69
  Palácio dos Marqueses da Fronteira, 95
  Palacio Nacional da Pena, 157
  Parque das Amoreiras, 74–75, 93
  Parque das Nações (Nations Park), 18, 20, 29, 32, 33, 163

Parque da Torre de
  Belém, 96
Parque Eduardo VII,
  4, 60–61, 90–91, 93
Parque Florestal de
  Monsanto, 94–96
Pedreira da Serafina, 95
Praça Marquês de
  Pombal, 60
Tagus Gardens Park, 33
Parque das Amoreiras,
  74–75, 93
Parque das Nações (Nations'
  Park), 18, 20, 29, 32,
  33, 163
Parque da Torre de Belém, 96
Parque do Tejo
  Playground, 33
Parque Eduardo VII,
  4, 60–61, 90–91, 93
Parque Florestal de
  Monsanto, 94–96
Passports, 168
Pavilhão Atlântico, 32, 124,
  127, 130
Pavilhão de Conhecimento
  (Knowledge Pavilion),
  17, 31
Pavilhão de Portugal (Portu-
  gal Pavilion), 18, 20, 28–29
Pedreira da Serafina, 95
Penha Longa Atlantic golf,
  155
Performing arts and enter-
  tainment, 14, 124–130
    best bets, 124
    classical music and con-
    cert venues, 127–128
    dance, 128
    film, 128–129
    fringe arts centers, 129
    maps, 125–126
    spectator sports,
    129–130
    theaters, 130
Pessoa, Fernando, 36, 39, 50
Peter Café Sport, 117
Pharmacies, 168–169
Picasso, Pablo, 46
Police, 169
Pomar, Julio, 50
Pombal, 36, 61
Ponte de Vasco da Gama
  (Vasco da Gama Bridge),
  18, 19, 29
Ponte 25 de Abril, 4, 29,
  35, 41
Port bars, 122
Portinari, Cândido, 49
Portugal Pavilion (Pavilhão de
  Portugal), 18, 20, 28–29

Portuguese language,
  54, 172–173
Postage, 168
Posto de Turismo, 158
Pottery, 83
Praça da Figueira, 25, 64
Praça das Armas, 53
Praça de Pedro IV, 25
Praça do Comércio, 3, 7, 8,
  25, 35, 61, 62
Praça do Império, 73
Praça dos Restauradores, 59
Praça Luis de Camões, 67–68
Praça Marquês de Pombal, 60
Pre-Reconquest Architec-
  ture, 23
Proença, Pedro, 20
Pubs. See Bars and pubs

Q
Quinta da Marinha Oitavos
  Golf, 155
Quinta da Regaleira, 159–160

R
Rato neighborhood, 74–76
Restaurants. See Dining
Restrooms, 170
Reveillon concert, 164
Rhizome (Antony
  Gormley), 20
Ribeiro, José Sommer, 48
Rio Vivo (Rolando Sá
  Nogueira), 20
River front, 72–73
Rock venues, 122
Rodin, August, 48
Rodrigues, Amália, 36, 37,
  61, 76, 91
Romantic locations, 40–43
Rossio Square, 9, 64–65
Rossio Station, 24, 65
Royal Palace, 53
Rua Augusta, 3, 7, 62, 63
Rua da Escola Politécnica, 69
Rua de São Bento, 76

S
Safety, 169
St Anthony festival, 162
Salazar, 35
Sales tax rebates, 87
Sá Nogueira, Rolando, 20
Santa Apolónia train
  station, 165
Santa Cruz, 42
Santos Design District, 3, 46
São Pedro de Alcântara, 4
Science and Natural History
  Museums, 69

Science museums
  Oceanário, 17–19, 31
  Pavilhão de Conheci-
    mento, 17, 31
  Science and Natural His-
    tory Museums, 69
Sé (Cathedral), 8–9, 23,
  56, 162
See Do Learn, 31
Segredo (Amália
  Rodrigues), 36
Shoe stores, 88
Shopping, 78–88
  for art and antiques, 82
  in Baixa, 63
  best bets, 78, 84
  for books, 82
  for carpets, 69
  for ceramics, pottery
    and tiles, 83
  for crafts and gifts,
    66, 86
  department stores and
    shopping centers,
    19, 20, 83, 84
  for fashion and acces-
    sories, 85–86, 88
  for furnishings and
    home goods, 84–85
  for gourmet food and
    drink, 64, 86–87
  for jewelry, 87
  maps, 79–81
  markets, 3, 66–67, 75, 84
  for music, 88
Sintra, 4, 33, 156–160
Sintra Festival of Music and
  Dance, 163
SL Benfica, 124
Smoking, 169
Soccer, 129–130, 163
Solar do Vinho do Porto,
  43, 112, 122
Sony Park, 32
Speakeasy Bar, 121–122
Special-interest tours, 22–50
  architecture, 22–29
  art museums and
    galleries, 44–50
  for children, 30–33
  Lisbon's heroes, 34–39
  romantic locations,
    40–43
Spectator sports, 129–130
Sports, 129–130
Squares
  Praça da Figueira, 25, 64
  Praça das Armas, 53
  Praça de Pedro IV, 25
  Praça do Comércio, 3,
    7, 8, 25, 35, 61, 62

Squares *(cont.)*
  Praça do Império, 73
  Praça dos Restauradores, 59
  Praça Luis de Camões, 67–68
  Praça Marquês de Pombal, 60
Stadiums
  Estádio da Luz, 129–130
  Estádio José de Alvalade, 130
  Estádio Nacional, 130, 162
  Pavilhão Atlântico, 32, 124, 127, 130
Superbock Superock festival, 163
Superliga soccer, 129–130, 163
Szenes, Arpad, 49

T

Tagus Gardens Park, 33
Tagus River, 4, 33, 41
Taverna d'El Rey, 120
Taxes, 169
Taxis, 165, 166
Teatro Camões, 124, 128
Teatro Nacional de Dona Maria II, 65, 124, 130
Teatro Nacional de São Carlos, 68, 124, 127–128
Teatro Politeama, 130
Teatro Politecnica, 69
Teatro São Luiz, 130
Teatro Tivoli, 130
Telephones, 169
Telmo, José Cotinelli, 15
Theaters
  Teatro Nacional de Dona Maria II, 65, 124, 130
  Teatro Nacional de São Carlos, 68, 124, 127–128
  Teatro Politeama, 130
  Teatro Politecnica, 69
  Teatro São Luiz, 130
  Teatro Tivoli, 130
Tiles, shopping for, 83
Timpanas, 120
Tipping, 169–170
Tivoli cinema, 60
Toilets, 170
Torre de Belém, 4, 14, 28, 71–72, 96, 164
Tourist information, 3, 7, 61, 96, 129, 140, 153, 168, 170
Trains, 18, 29, 153, 158, 165
Trams, 4, 7–8
Triumph Arch (Arco do Triunfo), 3, 7, 25, 62–63

Trumps club, 112, 120–121
Turismo de Lisboa, 129
25 de Abril Bridge, 4, 29, 35, 41

U

UCI Cinemas, 129
UNESCO World Heritage Sites, 14, 28, 71–72
The Unfinished House, 31

V

van der Kloet, Willem, 49
Vasco da Gama, 11, 36–39, 63
Vasco da Gama Bridge (Ponte Vasco da Gama), 18, 19, 29
Vasco da Gama shopping center, 31, 84
Vieira da Silva, Maria Helena, 48
Viera, Álvaro Siza, 29
Viera, Jorge, 20

W

Walking, 3, 52–76, 166
  in Alfama, 58–61
  in Baixa, 62–65
  in Belém, 70–73
  in Cais do Sodré, Chiado and Bairro Alto, 66–69
  in Rato, Amoreiras and Estrela, 74–76
Weather, 162, 164
Websites, useful, 162, 163
Wine, 64, 112, 122

Y

Yayoi-Kusama, 50

Z

Zoos, 32–33

Accommodations

Albergaria Senhora do Monte, 132, 138
Altis Belém Hotel, 72, 132, 138
As Janelas Verdes, 132, 138
Bairro Alto Hotel, 132, 138
Belmonte Hotel, 54
Corinthia Lisboa Hotel, 138
Duas Nações, 138, 139
Eden Teatro Aparthotel, 139, 140
Farol Design Hotel (Cascais), 153
Heritage Avenida Liberdade, 132, 140
Holiday Inn, 140

Hotel Altis, 140
Hotel Avenida Palace, 140–141
Hotel Britania, 141
Hotel Cascais Miragem, 153
Hotel Don Pedro, 141
Hotel Fénix, 141
Hotel Jerónimos 8, 132, 141
Hotel Lapa Palace, 132, 141–142
Hotel Mundial, 142
Hotel Olissippo Oriente, 142
Hotel Tivoli Lisboa, 142
Hotel Tivoli Tejo, 142
Hotel Trivoli Palácio de Seteais (Sintra), 159
Hotel Trivoli Sintra, 159
Hotel Tryp Oriente, 142–143
International Design Hotel, 143
Le Meridien Park Atlantic Lisbon, 91
Lisboa Tejo Hotel, 143
Mercure Lisboa, 143
Novotel, 132, 143–144
Palácio Belmonte, 132, 144
Penha Longa Golf & Hotel Resort (Sintra), 159
Pensão Residencial Princesa, 144
Pestana Palace Hotel, 144
Real Palácio Hotel, 144
Real Residencia Suite Hotel, 144
Residência Avenida Park, 132, 144
Residencial Dom Sancho I, 132, 144
Residencial Florescente, 144–145
Sheraton Lisboa Hotel & Spa, 132, 145
Sofitel, 132, 145
Solar do Castelo Heritage Hotel, 54, 145
Travellers House Hostel, 132, 146
VIP Executive Barcelona Hotel, 132, 146
VIP Veneza Hotel, 146
York House Hotel, 146

Restaurants

A Brasileira, 39, 98, 103
A Commenda, 103
Alcântara Café, 103
Amoreiras Shopping Center, 75
Antiga Confeitaria de Belém, 11, 98, 103
Bica do Sapato, 103
Café Luso, 3

Café Martinho da Arcada, 35, 98, 103–104
Café Nicola, 104
Café Quadrante, 13, 104
CAMJAP Restaurant, 48
Casa México, 104
Cervejaria da Trindade, 27, 98, 105
Cervejaria Portugália, 72, 73, 98, 105
Chapitô, 53
Charcutaria Brasil, 74
Chimarrã, 105
Claras em Castelo, 98, 106
Clube de Fado, 57
Comida da Ribeira, 66
Confeitaria Nacional, 64
Cozinha Velha (Sintra), 159
Dragão do Alfama, 106

Estufa Real, 98, 106
Feitoria, 98, 106–107
Gambrinus, 98, 107
Ginjinha, 65
Jardim do Marisco, 107
Ja Sei, 72
La Rúcula, 31, 107
Manifesto, 98, 107
Martinho da Arcada, 61
Nariz do Vinho Tinto, 98, 107–108
Nicola, 64
Nood, 108
Nune's Real Marisqueira, 98, 108
Olivier Avenida, 108
O Regional, 108–109
Pastelaria Suiça, 64, 109
Pateo do Garrett (Sintra), 159

Real Indiana, 109
Restaurante Ad-Lib, 98, 109
Restaurante Búfalo Grill, 109
Restaurante Casa do Leão, 42
Restaurante Eleven, 61, 98, 106
Restaurante Faz Figura, 110
Restaurante Las Brasitas, 110
Restaurante Marisqueira Quebra Mar, 110
Restaurante Pap'Açorda, 110
Restaurante Quebra-Mar, 60
Restaurante Senhor Peixe, 110
Restaurante Tavares, 39, 98, 110
Rua do Bojador, 19
Santíssimus, 98, 110
Suiça, 64

Photo **Credits**

Notes

Explore over 3,500 destinations.

Frommers.com makes it easy.

Find a destination. ✓ Book a trip. ✓ Get hot travel deals.
Buy a guidebook. ✓ Enter to win vacations. ✓ Listen to podcasts.
Check out the latest travel news. ✓ Share trip photos and memories.
And much more.

Frommers.com